COMMON
SENSE
SELF
DEFENSE

COMMON SENSE SELF DEFENSE

by
Carl Hausman
Chris Dakas

Published by
Leather Stocking Books
Pine Mountain Press, Inc. Publishing Group
P.O. Box 13604
Wauwatosa, WI 53226

CREDITS

Editor: *Marilyn A. Brilliant, M.S.*
Typesetting: *The Graphic Worx, ltd.*
Production & Printing: *ARCATA*

Table Of Contents

Preface

You are holding what we feel will be an extremely effective book—which is, of course, why we wrote it. We want to tell you right away what this book is about and why it will be valuable.

Many of the self defense books on the market today are unrealistic in their approach and ignore techniques of preventing trouble. On the other hand, most of the books which focus on crime prevention contain barely a mention of how to defend yourself. It has become obvious that a combination of the two is vital for people concerned about their safety and the safety of their families.

Common Sense Self Defense is written with this two-pronged approach. It contains a variety of simple, effective karate techniques which can be adapted to various situations. Methods of avoiding trouble are stressed throughout the book, including chapters written specifically for senior citizens, women, and parents of young children. Also included is a complete guide for security in the home. Weapons, their pluses and minuses, are discussed, too.

These are things you need to know, but which you probably won't be told in typical self defense or crime prevention books. Perhaps, though, you might wonder if the emphasis we place on restraint in using self defense techniques and the need for avoiding danger reflects some sort of soft approach toward crime and criminals. That's not the case.

Let's state our philosophy about this issue right at the beginning, so you can decide whether or not this book is for you. We present all points of view and as many sides of the situation as possible because you need a wide variety of strategies in your self defense arsenal. We believe you should avoid trouble when you can because a physical confrontation is just too much of a hassle. But no one has the right to harm you. You should meet force with force if you are physically able, and use what you feel is an appropriate level of violence in your response.

When you fight back, you must not do so half-heartedly. The only way you'll be able to utilize self defense tactics is if you make up your mind that there may come a time when you must *hurt* your attacker. Hit him as *hard* as you can. If your life is in danger, maim, cripple or kill if you have to—if you think you could live with the results.

That's the realistic kind of approach needed to deal with the complex subject of self defense. We will teach you how to avoid trouble if possible and protect yourself if you can't avoid it.

Carl Hausman
Chris Dakas

Introduction

• George is a tourist—quite obviously a tourist—on his way through a part of New York City he really never intended to visit. After getting mixed up on the subway, George and his wife began walking back toward their hotel, unaware that they were heading into a high crime area. Now, only one thing is on George's mind: the three hundred dollars in vacation money stuffed into his wallet. He reaches back repeatedly, nervously patting the bulge in his back pocket, thinking of all the stories he's heard about New York pickpockets. Suddenly, a young man in a leather jacket steps out from a doorway and touches the tip of a long, thin knife to George's throat. "Hand over the cash," he says, "or you get cut."

• Ted, a college student, always gets nervous walking to his night class. The campus is located in an urban area, and at night the neighborhood becomes thick with what the students call the "derelict squad." Tonight, a large, tough-looking denizen of the street takes an aggressive approach toward collecting for his next bottle. "All right, sonny," he slurs, "how about a contribution to my retirement fund?" Ted reacts in fright and anger, screaming threats and obscenities. His assailant, squinting through an alcoholic haze, reacts by swinging his half-empty wine bottle at Ted's head.

Scenes like these are repeated every day of the week, in every major city in the United States. Through a basic lack of knowledge about crime and criminals, many citizens inadvertently place themselves in dangerous positions. And through lack of experience and judgement, they often find themselves unable to handle a crisis situation—incapable of reacting quickly, of giving the correct verbal, physical and psychological response.

Our friend George the Tourist, for example, didn't realize that his nervous habit of patting his wallet would draw criminals like flies. Streetwise attackers don't just notice the wallet-patting habit, you see, they actively look for it. They've learned to recognize the body language of people who are uncomfortable about carrying large amounts of cash.

Sometimes, trouble can't be avoided. Ted, the student, couldn't help where and when he had to attend classes. Unfortunately, Ted reacted exactly the wrong way when the drunk grabbed him. Because of his lack of experience, Ted didn't realize that when dealing with a drunken and probably deranged assailant, words are not the answer.

The response must be physical. Had Ted used one of the hand techniques explained in Chapter 3, he could have broken the drunk's grip, used a basic leverage hold to pull him off balance, and walked away briskly.

But words can be the right answer, depending on the situation; later on we'll explore time-tested ways to defuse a potentially violent situation. What would you do, for instance, if you were in an unsavory neighborhood and accidentaly bump into an equally unsavory fellow who turns a corner quickly? The best bet—the response most likely to calm the situation—would be a short, dignified apology. Your mortified silence might be construed as an indication that you simply don't care that you jostled a passerby. If that's what the street tough thinks, you might be in for trouble.

Common Sense Self Defense is written to help you recognize that best bet, the best option in a dangerous situation. In some cases, a physical confrontation can be avoided by the right word, the right response, the right attitude. Sometimes, quick and effective physical action might be the only alternative; it might take the form of a punch, a hold, or a throw. Perhaps—but only with full knowledge of the possible consequences—your reaction might involve use of a weapon.

This book takes a realistic approach toward self defense. Practical martial arts techniques will be presented in a simplified format with a clear sequence of photos. Weapons, their uses and drawbacks, will be discussed. Most importantly, *Common Sense Self Defense* will explain the importance of self confidence, an attitude proven to be vital through years of experience in the streets and in the gym.

There are no guarantees, and you should be skeptical of anyone who offers a pat solution to a complex situation. But *Common Sense Self Defense* will give you, at the very least, a fighting chance.

Chapter 1

What Are My Chances?

Crime statistics in the United States contain, as in the all-too-familiar joke, some good news and some bad news. The good news is that your chances of avoiding violent crime are probably better than you think. Although statistical studies are often complex and even misleading, one general observation seems to hold true: Mathematically, the odds against your being attacked are high, quite high.

Now, the bad news: There's a steadily swelling increase in stranger-to-stranger crime, and this is a dangerous trend for an average citizen. Many of the violent crimes that comprise the statistics have traditionally been committed among people who know each other. But stranger-to-stranger crime—the type we seem to fear most—is random and unpredictable. So while you may not come from a socio-economic environment where you fear attacks from acquaintances or family members, you do face an ever-increasing threat of street crime.

Even the statistical measure of safety you enjoy on

11

paper is flawed, too. If the improbable happens—just a once-in-a-lifetime attack, let's say—your life may be changed forever. Physical injuries may, in severe cases, last for years. The emotional scars are less quick to heal. Years later, the memory of a violent attack may still be fresh, and the victim haunted by fear.

Remember, too, that a person victimized once is likely to be victimized again. A mugger who gets $200 from a man walking to work is certain to keep an eye out for that same fellow in the weeks, months, or years to come. More importantly, someone terrorized by a first attack begins to *look and act like a victim*. People, like dogs, can instinctively sense fear. In effect, the fear of an attack may provoke one.

This is precisely the reason why we are stressing the point that the *perceived* danger of attack is often greater than the actual danger; in other words, physical confrontations are not as common as you might think. However, if you are consumed by a fear of crime, *it shows*, making an attack more likely.

Don't assume, though, that crime is not a real danger. It is, and the problem appears to be growing worse. Preparing to defend yourself against physical crime is logical and sensible. The feeling of self confidence you are likely to develop along the way will do nothing but help you in all other aspects of life.

Despite what you may have been led to believe by the violent antics of martial arts movies, attitude is the key to self defense. Physical prowess alone, without the benefit of sound judgement and common sense, is sometimes worse than useless. (Note how often the man with the big fists and the belligerent personality winds up a shooting victim; not only was he powerless to stop the attack, he almost certainly brought it upon himself.)

The ultimate goal of this book is to help you overcome fear. By overcoming fear (changing your attitude, in other words) you'll be able to react quickly and effectively when confronted with violence. You will also have the presence of mind to think clearly, without having your mind and body paralyzed by panic. How do you learn to conquer fear? In the beginning, you'll probably look toward an external measure to reinforce your courage. Carrying a weapon is one alternative, although a weapon can often be more trouble than it's worth (this will be discussed in **Chapter 8 and 9**). Perhaps you may opt to lift weights, get your body in shape, making yourself a less attractive target. Many people find that developing a proficiency in the martial arts is the most appealing avenue to a new, self-assured personality.

Don't forget that your newly-developing self confidence must be augmented by common sense, the ability to avoid trouble. Unfortunately, most "solid citizens," who have no experience with crime and criminals, might not realize why they are making themselves tempting targets.

George, the tourist type mentioned in the introduction, didn't realize that his nervous habit of patting a bulging wallet was tantamount to carrying a sign saying "mug me." So before we begin exploring the martial arts, let's first examine some common-sense methods of avoiding trouble before it brews:

- *Don't become raucus in places where you are a stranger.* If you're coming out of a restaurant in an unfamiliar neighborhood and encounter a group of surly teenagers loitering on the corner, now is not the time to start bragging loudly to your date about your mountain climbing abilities. Remember that some people will regard you with hostility just because you are a stranger, and drawing attention to yourself only makes matters worse. Also, you may unknowingly break some unspoken rule, playing on "the gang's" pinball machine, for instance.
- *Don't dress in clothing or jewelry which will attract attention.* If some unavoidable errand takes you to a bad neighborhood, try not to wear a three piece suit. You will undoubtedly stir hostility and give the impression of having money. Flashy jewelry has the same effect; if you must walk through a high-crime area, and can't bring yourself to leave your finery at home in the bureau drawer, at least keep it out of sight. Tuck

necklaces inside your blouse or sweater when traveling, and pull them out when you arrive at dinner. Flashy watches should be pushed up the wrist out of sight under the cuff, and expensive-looking rings placed in pockets.

- *Project a good image of yourself.* Don't look like a victim. Let's face it, some people just ooze susceptibility, and the nervous-looking fellow slinking down the street glancing over his shoulder is setting himself up for trouble. He may appeal to:
  a. The malicious type of assailant who seeks gratification from bullying others and is looking for an easy target, a "sheep."
  b. A robber whose primary concern is money. To this type of criminal, the victim's furtive manner may indicate he's carrying something valuable.[1]

In the effort to project a good image, don't adopt a surly, tough-guy attitude, either. Swaggering down the street making eye contact with every passerby will eventually cause trouble. Your goal is to appear *alert* and *comfortable.*

An alert person is obviously not the first choice of a prospective mugger, who would like to depend on the element of surprise. A person comfortable in his surroundings does not present an attractive target, either. "He might be a cop," a thief might think. Or "She doesn't look worried...I wonder if she has a lot of friends in this neighborhood?"

- *Remember that heavy drug and alcohol use precipitates violence and mars judgement.* Alcohol and drugs release inhibitions, and can trigger attacks based on nothing else than the fact that the fellow across the bar doesn't like the color of your hair. If you, too, are drunk or stoned or otherwise insensible, you may find yourself without the judgement or physical ability to handle the situation. So if you feel the need to occasionally blow out the cobwebs, you're better off doing it at home with a group of friends.
- *Pay attention to your instincts.* If your antennae start to tingle, don't try to discount the feeling. Man is, after all, an animal, and still possesses surprisingly accurate intuition.

Unfortunately, caution and good judgement won't always be sufficient to head off an attack on your person. When such an attack looms, self confidence, a cool head and a decisive plan of action are vital. These qualities are all part of that mysterious and intriguing field we call the martial arts.

---

1. Keep in mind that an armed criminal whose sole intent is robbing your money—if he believes you have quite a bit of it—may strike regardless of your image. He might, for that matter, choose a victim who is seven feet tall and can crush coconuts. For this reason, the best defense against this type of assailant is avoidance: not putting yourself in a position to be robbed and/or not looking like you have something worth taking. But even this strategy is not foolproof.

Chapter 2

Fighting Back: The Martial Arts

If karate were practiced today the way it was in the sixteenth century, there would be a law against it. The techniques developed by karate's originators, Chinese monks in need of a way to defend themselves against armed attackers, were quick, decisive and deadly. Their stances were patterned after the fighting positions of animals, and their movements were no-nonsense affairs: crushing the windpipe, gouging an eye, smashing the groin. Admittedly, it was a brutal art, but those were brutal times, and the goal was survival, pure and simple.

When the Chinese monks developed their fighting system, their particular martial art, it was known as *kung fu,* meaning, literally, hard work. Kung fu spread to other parts of the Orient, becoming *karate* in Okinawa. Karate translates to *empty hand.* The art eventually spread to Japan, and after WWII, to the United States via returning GIs. Today, of course, karate is a sport and part of the Oriental culture.

15

In Okinawa, for example, karate is part of the overall philosophy of life. The Oriental lifestyle supports anything which has a strong cultural or educational benefit to the society. And although karate is really not regarded as a religion, most masters would no more think of commercializing the art than a Catholic priest would consider selling blessings.

This isn't the case in the United States. Karate is big business because of its appeal to the media and to the American imagination. The prospect of subduing an attacker with a quick chop surely appeals to the same sort of frontier psychology which fostered the quick draw. (Note how judo, a less spectacular martial art which focuses heavily on trips and arm-bending, never really caught on when it hit Occidental shores.)

Because the American concept of karate often differs significantly from reality, many people are misled and, indeed, endangered. The famous Bill Cosby comedy routine (where he finishes his karate course and walks around with ten dollar bills hanging from his pockets because he can't wait to be attacked) is not all that fanciful. Plenty of graduates of the local "ten easy lessons" karate emporium have been given a dangerous dose of overconfidence and have learned their lesson the hard way.

The myth of invincibility is dangerous, extremely dangerous, and should be debunked right from the outset of the karate training included in this book. Although there's no question that karate techniques can be very effective in self defense situations, always remember that no one is invincible—regardless of his or her skill in the martial arts. And for someone who has only a basic grounding in karate, ignoring danger or actively courting it is an act of stupidity (not to mention a violation of the basic precepts of the martial arts). So if, after two weeks of practice, you feel the need to enter the neighborhood bar and brag about your newly-found martial arts abilities, don't be too surprised if you fall victim to a well-placed beer bottle to the head; you won't be the first person it's happened to.

Before moving on to basic karate stances and exercises, let's consider another point which is a major factor in the application of karate techniques to street situations: Do you have the nerve to use it? Remember, karate can be brutally effective. A movement which crushes your assailant's windpipe will undoubtedly put an end to the attack, but some people simply could never bring themselves to take this kind of action, even if they believed they were in a life-or-death situation.

There is no disgrace in this attitude, because it takes a rational and mature person to hold a high regard for life, even the life of an attacker. Likewise, there is certainly no disgrace in avoiding violence. Fighting is undoubtedly the lowest form of human interaction; if it can be avoided, you have struck a blow for human dignity.

However, the choice between running and fighting is not always clear-cut, and no one can spell out a formula for determining when to back off and when to stand your ground.

In some cases, you may be able to intelligently talk your way out of a situation. Methods of doing this will be discussed in **Chapter 15**. Often, raising your voice may calm the situation if your attacker is yelling at you—he may just be blustering, and have no desire to escalate the confrontation after your show of force. There's no canned solution, but your instincts may prove to be the determining factor; they are the best guide you will have in most situations, so you must learn to pay attention to them and trust your judgement.

The only hard-and-fast rule about dealing with a potentially violent conflict is to maintain your balance and be ready for action. Assuming the correct *on-guard* stance has two advantages: it puts you in a position where you can respond quickly and it gives you a psychological edge by presenting yourself as a calm individual who is not showing fright or aggression. Note that the on-guard stance is not a fighting stance with fists upraised, but rather a relaxed and confident posture.

Assume the on-guard stance by placing your feet shoulder-width apart, one foot pulled slightly back. A right-handed person will generally feel more comfortable with the right foot drawn back. A left-hander may wish to reverse some of the stances and movements shown in this book. Shoulders should be level—the right one no higher or lower than the left—with the right shoulder drawn back slightly. Bend the knees slightly. Hands should be crossed in front of you with a loose grip. Don't fold your arms across the chest, since it will hamper your ability to defend yourself and give an antagonist a negative body-language signal.

This balanced, relaxed on-guard stance will be your basic starting point for many of the movements shown in this book. During an actual combat situation—if you have time—you will naturally want to adopt a fighting stance. Don't however, go into the fighting stance until you absolutely have to, or you may actually provoke a fight.

The on-guard stance.

The fighting stance for a right-handed person. The position may be reversed for a left-hander.

The hands are held in the fist position in the basic fighting stance, although more advanced techniques to be demonstrated later will involve grabbing with an open hand. The arms are now in a position to strike and parry. The right foot is drawn back slightly farther than in the on-guard stance.

Because a proper stance is basic to any self defense maneuver, it's important to make sure that you're doing it correctly from the beginning. Mistakes, with practice, will become bad habits. The best option is to have an experienced karate teacher, or *sensei*, check your position.[1] Barring that, assume your stance and take this self-check test:

☐ Are my feet shoulder-width apart, with my weight equally distributed?
☐ Are my knees bent slightly?
☐ Do I feel well balanced, cat-like?
☐ Are my shoulders level?
☐ Is my back straight?
☐ Are my head and neck straight, without my face drooping forward and presenting an easy target?

The position may at first seem unnatural, even tiring. Muscles in the legs may rebel initially, since they are rarely asked to flex into a springy position. And if you are feeling a bit sore from simply assuming the stance, imagine the shape you'd be in after practicing a few high kicks designed to strike your opponent's jaw!

Fortunately, you don't have to reconcile yourself to a future of aches, pains and pulled muscles. The body has a marvelous ability to adapt to new activities—and that's the goal of a moderate exercise program. The kind of workout practiced in karate will prepare you to perform karate movements and improve your general fitness. Being fit, in turn, will improve your appearance and boost your self confidence.

---

1. There's no reason why you can't combine techniques explained in this book with formal martial arts training. In fact, the combination would be quite effective. After reading this book, you'll have enough of a basic introduction to the martial arts to help you decide what kind of advanced training to pursue.

We'll demonstrate a workout program before proceeding with self defense techniques. This routine should be practiced every other day or so, and is especially valuable as a warmup before practicing actual techniques. You may wish to alternate this workout with a light running program. As you progress, you may add additional repetitions to the movements. You should also aim for improving your form in the exercises — you may at first have to cheat a little, but as you get in better shape try to do the movements perfectly. Let's start at the bottom:

1. Stand barefoot, bend forward, grasp the toes and pull upward.

    Release your grip, stand up, and—using one foot at a time—curl your toes so that the foot creeps forward.

This exercise is important to help prevent injury to the foot, which can occur even when you kick while wearing a shoe.

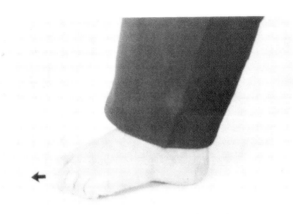

Curl the toes so that the foot creeps forward.

This movement will strengthen the feet and help you assume some of the rather difficult foot positions called for in karate. Repeat this movement five to ten times.

2. Lift one foot off the floor and flex the toes. Move your foot through a complete range of motion, twisting clockwise and counterclockwise. Twist each foot ten times.

3. Hold both kneecaps in the palms of your hands and rotate the kneecaps gently with circular motions of your hands. Massage the kneecaps throughout this movement. Now, slowly drop to a squatting position with the knees facing forward. Come back to a standing position, continuing the circular massaging motion of hands on knees. Repeat this movement five to ten times.

4. Next, do the same movement but draw the knees apart as you lower yourself; bring the knees together as you approach the floor. (see pages 24-26.)

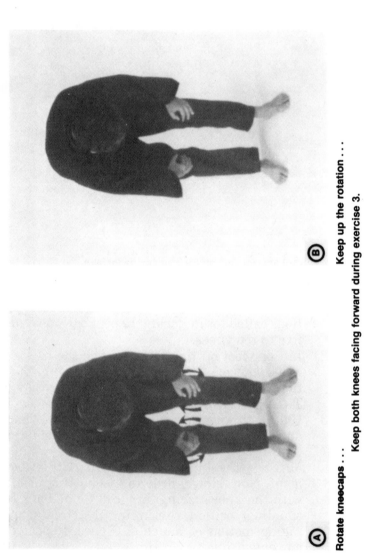

Ⓐ Rotate kneecaps . . .

Ⓑ Keep up the rotation . . .

Keep both knees facing forward during exercise 3.

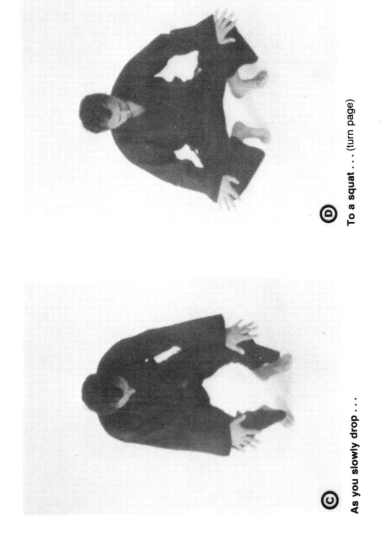

C As you slowly drop . . .

D To a squat . . . (turn page)

Repeat this process as you rise. Bring your knees apart into the frog position by the time you are halfway up. Knees will naturally come together as you rise fully upright. Repeat five times, but increase the repetitions as you get better at this movement, working up to ten repetitions.

5. This exercise will add further suppleness to the knees.

   Stand upright, and use the same circular motion to rotate the knees. Now, reverse the motion of your hands as they massage the knees—clockwise, counterclockwise and clockwise again. Do this for a minute or so.

6. Ready for a really tough one? Extend hands in front of you, spread legs as far as you can and lower yourself onto the right buttock, extending the left leg. From this position, shift to the left

Then return to a standing position continuing the massage of the kneecaps.

Exercise 6, first position. Lower the body onto the right buttock.

Exercise 6, second position. Shift onto the left buttock, extending the right leg . . . .

buttock, extending the right leg. Do not come up and down but stay close to the floor in this exercise. Go from right to left five to ten times. This can be done with the inner edge of the foot touching the floor or with just the heel touching, which is more difficult. Start with the side of the foot and eventually progress to the heel.

7. The pushup is unequaled as a builder of arm and chest strength. Keep the body straight, lower yourself until the chest touches the ground, then push back up.

When you get more advanced, try doing pushups off the first and second knuckles of your fists. But first read Chapter 3 to make sure that you are forming the fist properly. Start with ten pushups, but as you progress do as many as you feel

If standard pushups like these are too difficult, try putting your knees on the floor.

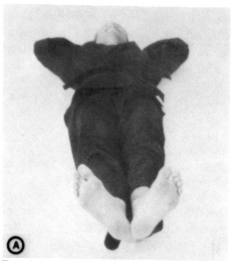

Exercise 8, first position.

you can handle.

8. Lie on your back and lace fingers behind the head. Keeping legs straight, lift heels about six inches off the floor. Keeping knees locked, gently bounce the legs ten times from the hips.

   Now, spread the legs half of their full spread, bouncing another ten times (facing page).

   Make sure not to touch heels to floor. Next, repeat this movement with the legs spread far apart (page 32). Finish off by doing ten more at half-spread and ten with knees together.

9. Tighten neck muscles by drawing the mouth and jaw into a grimace. Move the head slowly in a nodding motion.

   After going through the nodding motion 5 to 10 times, take a couple of minutes and roll the head through a full range of motion, clockwise and counterclockwise, as shown on page 33.

   Don't be surprised if you yawn during this motion; it's a very relaxing exercise.

Exercise 8, second position. Spread legs half of full spread.

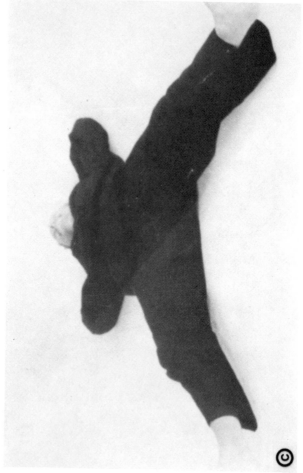

Exercise 8, third position, with legs at full spread.

Rolling the head through clockwise and counterclockwise motions loosens and limbers the neck.

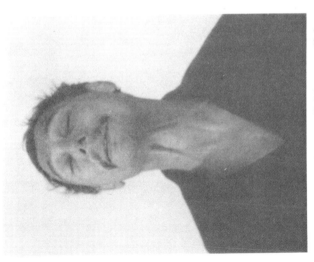

Strong neck muscles are vital in any self defense situation. It's often not the contact to the head that causes injury from a blow — it's the snapping of an unconditioned neck. Here, the neck muscles are tightened by grimacing.

After a couple sessions of this routine, you will begin to notice an increase in flexibility (and a decrease in the stiffness you probably felt after your first workout).

Now you're ready to move into the first set of karate movements: the basic hand techniques.

Chapter 3

Karate Hand Techniques

One basic principle of karate might have been taught to you during high school math: The shortest distance between two points is a straight line. It's this principle which guides the way that karate punches are thrown. They are short, snappy and powerful.

A good punch doesn't have to be thrown from six feet behind you. While a looping roundhouse might be a good punch for a boxer who has his opponent on the ropes, it is not the preferred technique for self defense, since it takes too much time to execute and leaves you vulnerable while winding up.

Punching will be dealt with in this chapter even though it is not technically part of *hand techniques*, which involve diverting an opponent's blow with your own hands and arms (by means of blocking and parrying); and grips, which exert leverage on your attacker's hands and wrists. The punch is often the concluding act

35

of a hand technique, a sequence which will be explained later in the chapter.

The first step in throwing a proper punch is learning the correct way to form a fist. This is very important in street situations, because an improper fist can lead to hand and wrist injury. An injured hand could leave you virtually defenseless.

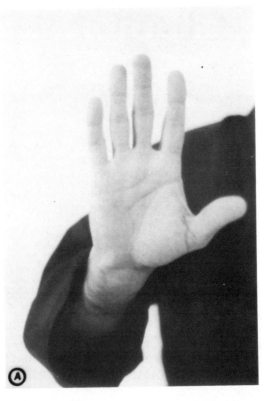

A properly made fist prevents hand and wrist injury. To form a proper fist . . .

Common Sense Self Defense

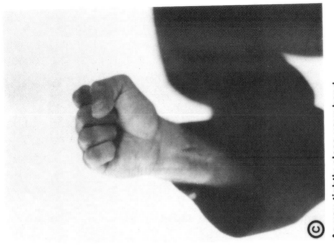

As you tightly close your hand.

Roll the fingers tightly so that you can feel the flesh of your palm bunch up . . .

To make a fist, first roll the fingers tightly, then close the fist so that the flesh of the palm is bunched. Don't just rest the fingers loosely in the palm. If you can't feel the flesh of the palm bunched underneath the fingertips, the fist is not made properly. The thumb is then placed safely alongside the fingers as shown in the photos on the previous page.

The fist becomes a weapon when the proper motion of the body propels it at your opponent. Bear in mind that the instinctive way you throw a punch is not necessarily the correct way, just as the instinctive way to swing a golf club is not proper form, either. Remember how awkward the first few golf swings felt, as you were instructed to "keep the right elbow in and the head down?" Well, if you practiced, the merit of this initially uncomfortable form became self-evident, as the ball traveled much farther than it would have if you swung the club in instinctive, baseball-bat style.

By the same token, correct punching form may at first seem awkward, but through practice it will become natural, quick and powerful.

The starting position for the punch involves the elbow close in at the side—not flaring out like a wing. Keeping the elbow close to the body may be difficult to master at first, but the position will add to the velocity of the punch by eliminating any wasted motion.

Note from the photos that the fist turns down as the elbow passes the body; it turns over completely by the time the punch lands. Also note that the wrist stays rigid, directly in line with the upper arm, straight as a ruler. This is critical to the proper execution of a punch, because any bend in the wrist will expose it to injury.

The punching motion is something like the action of a piston. A piston, of course, moves in a cylinder in a straight line. Any excess motion would deplete power. As you practice the karate punch, you'll begin to feel the inherent power in this short, direct punching mo-

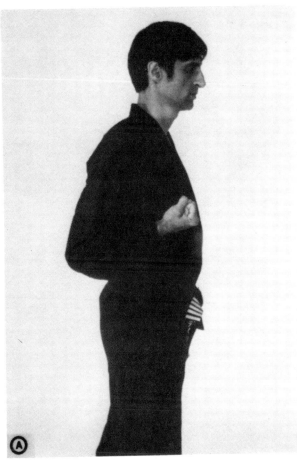

Note how the wrist stays absolutely straight throughout the punching motion. (turn page)

When the elbow passes the body.

During the punch, the fist will turn . . .

tion, and the movement will soon feel more natural. Practice by throwing punches into the air (remember to practice punching with both hands), or carefully punch a soft object such as a mattress or mat placed against a wall.

As mentioned earlier, the punch is generally the concluding act of a hand technique. Let's now examine the sequence.

A hand technique consists of:
1. The preliminary act
2. The technique itself
3. The concluding act: a punch, throw or hold which can disable the assailant or otherwise end the attack.

Here's how this three-pronged motion might work in a street situation. Suppose a hostile individual makes a grab for your shirt, as shown below.

The preliminary act—in this case, a block to keep an attacker from grabbing your shirt.

The first step, the preliminary act, is a motion to keep your attacker from grabbing you. (It should be noted that a novice to the martial arts will most likely be at a disadvantage once grabbed; experts, though can sometimes turn being grabbed into an advantage.) This is an elementary blocking motion, which involves nothing more intricate than deflecting the attacker's hand before it reaches your shirt. Some more advanced blocking motions—useful in warding off punches and kicks—will be demonstrated later in this chapter.

To summarize so far: the block is the preliminary act in a hand technique. It is followed by the technique itself.

In this case, the technique involves a twisting motion of the attacker's hand. Because of the tremendous leverage exerted by this hand-gripping and twisting technique, it causes a great deal of pain and drives the opponent off balance.

The hand technique starts by grabbing the hand you've blocked . . .

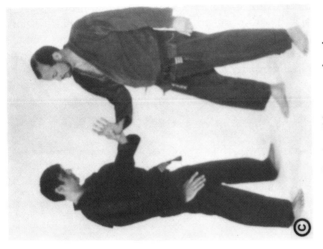

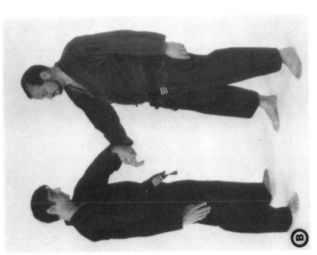

The hand technique involves grasping the hand and thumb. To be effective, this or any hand technique must be preceded by a preliminary act and followed by a concluding act. In this case, the concluding act (which will be shown on page 46 and 47) takes advantage of the fact that the pressure exerted in the above hand technique forces your opponent to lean backwards.

The technique shown on the previous pages is accomplished by placing your palm over the back of the opponent's hand, grasping the hand firmly, and twisting in the manner shown. The technique shown below involves twisting in the opposite direction.

Again, the hand technique is preceded by a block, and your attacker's hand is grasped . . .

If the hand is twisted in this direction . . . .

The opponent is forced to lean forward.

From the photographs (or from gentle experimentation with a partner) note how the pressure on the wrist affects the opponent's balance. In the first illustration of the hand-twisting technique, (page 43) the opponent was forced to lean backward in order to take some of the pressure off his wrist. In the second set of photos, where the twisting motion is reversed, (page 45) he is forced to lean forward.

This off-balance position (leaning either forward or backward) is exploited in your concluding act. When the twisting grip is such that the opponent is leaning backward, use your free hand to push against his hand; the pressure will drive him to the ground.

The concluding act to the hand technique which twists the hand this way is shown on the facing page.

Take advantage of your opponent being off balance by pushing on the hand and forcing him to the ground. This is the concluding act to the hand technique which forces the opponent to lean backward.

When you have twisted the attacker's hand in such a fashion that he's forced to lean forward, take advantage of his off-balance position by grabbing with your hand and pulling forward, forcing the arm—and the attached attacker—to the ground.

Ⓐ

The concluding act of the hand technique which forces the opponent to lean forward starts from this position . . .

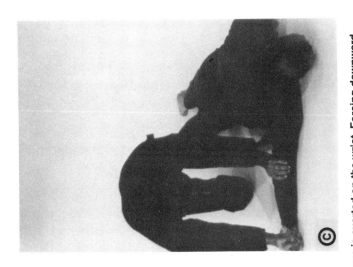

Then, the opponent is pulled to the ground as pressure is exerted on the wrist. Forcing downward on the elbow will add to the effect.

What we've seen is a relatively complex movement with variations for twisting the attacker's hand in either direction. The two variations were demonstrated in hopes that you'll begin to see and feel the amount of leverage which can be generated by a proper technique *and* understand the importance of a proper follow-up once the opponent is off balance. It's vital that this concept be grasped before we proceed any farther in the martial arts. To make sure that you understand the mechanics of both variations, let's watch them from beginning to end.

Since this is the first movement demonstrated for defense against an attacker, it's wise to remark at this point about the value of practicing with a partner. It is extremely difficult to develop proficiency in karate movement unless you practice it with a living, breathing human. ("Shadowboxing" against an imaginary opponent is also a valuable exercise, especially in trying to prepare for and anticipate various street situations, but practicing solo won't help you understand such factors as balance and body mechanics.)

It's not necessary—or advisable—to engage in brutal, rough-and-tumble sessions; even a husband and wife or parent and child can use this book as a practice guide to mastering basic techniques. The important thing is to gently work with your partner to learn how the movements work. Use discretion and judgement to prevent injury.

The twisting technique was demonstrated first because it shows graphically *how to follow up on an advantage.* You'll recall that the concluding act of each technique involved forcing the opponent to the ground. You'll recall, too, that the concluding act you chose depended on the situation. If the technique had the attacker leaning backward, you used a concluding act that put further pressure in the direction your opponent was leaning.

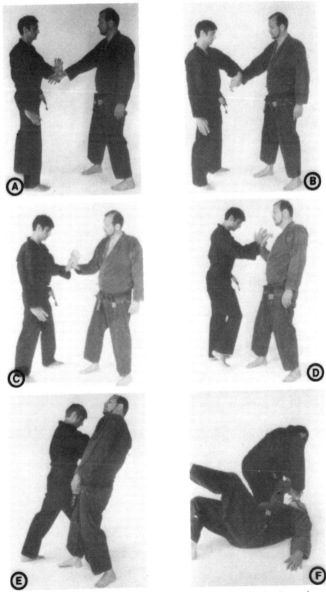

The hand technique which drives the opponent backward.

The hand technique which pulls the opponent forward.

This particular technique would be useful in a situation where you felt reasonably sure that our attacker—once he finds himself on the ground—would reconsider the wisdom of continuing the attack. In a case where you believe the attacker is intent on doing you serious injury, a more vigorous concluding act might be in order—a disabling punch or kick, for example. Remember, though, that if you throw a punch in response to a grab, you have in effect "raised the stakes." If the punch doesn't immediately disable the attacker, you will probably have a fistfight on your hands.

On the other side of the coin, if the assailant is violently angry, demented, or intent on doing you serious harm, you may have accomplished little by twisting his wrist, other than making him angrier.

What's the answer? Unfortunately, there is no answer which applies in every case. When deciding how much force to use, you must listen to your instincts. If you feel in your gut that you can end an attack without injuring the aggressive person, you may be able to end the situation simply, without escalating the matter. In the initial stages, you may be able to talk your way out of trouble, which is a very valuable technique to be discussed in Chapter 15.

Don't however, try to talk your way out of trouble if the situation has already become violent. Generally, physical force should always be met with physical force. Once someone is actually inflicting injury on you, the time for conversation is over.

If the situation involves someone throwing a punch at you, you will want to meet the attack with roughly equal force. Equal force does not mean responding to a punching assailant by gently trying to pin him to the ground. Nor does it mean using a technique which will kill or cripple him.

Next, we'll examine a technique which meets a punch with equal force: the sidestep, pull and strike.

The sidestep, pull and strike technique. The sidestep, pull and strike is effective when someone is directing a wild, lunging punch at you. The sidestep is pictured above. Photos B and C on the facing page show . . .

And the strike. Other types of strikes could be used, but this method — a blow to the nose with the edge of the hand near the thumb — works well in this situation.

The pull . . .

55

Remember the sequence of *preliminary act,* the *technique itself,* and the *concluding* act? The sequence holds true in the sidestep, pull and strike, too.

The preliminary act involves sidestepping the punch, which is not easy but can be done without extreme difficulty when the punch is a long "haymaker." In this preliminary act, you step to the outside, moving so the attacker's arm swings between his body and yours. Since moving to the inside and outside are commonly used terms, let's digress a moment to illustrate the distinction. The photo below shows movement to the outside. A movement to the inside is shown on the facing page.

Stepping to the outside of a punch.

Stepping to the inside of a punch.

Although boxers prefer to step to the inside of a punch giving them opportunity to throw punches to the body, the safest movement for beginners in karate usually involves stepping to the outside. Remember that you have more tools at your command than a boxer: you can feel free to grab, pull, kick and trip, and these movements are generally more easily accomplished when you have stepped outside and given yourself room to maneuver.

Now, getting back to the sidestep, pull and strike: After the preliminary act of sidestepping, the technique itself involves pulling the opponent off balance. Pulling really isn't the best description, perhaps; you want the attacker's momentum to do most of the work, so the technique ideally won't involve more than a light grip on the wrist, guiding the opponent off balance. By not tugging violently on the arm, you don't run the risk of putting yourself off balance.

Notice how the right hand is in a perfect position to strike the assailant's face. The back of the neck will also be exposed, but striking this area can cause serious injury and should usually be reserved for an attack where your life is threatened (see Chapter 7, which deals with deadly force). The strike with the free hand, of course, constitutes the concluding act.

Where do you aim a strike or punch? Generally, try to strike the face below the nose. A punch aimed above the nose may wind up bouncing off your attacker's skull, doing little damage—except to your hand, perhaps. Punches to the body can be effective but are often difficult to land properly.

Remember that in a street situation, you may be hard-pressed to land a punch, period. Trying to pinpoint a vulnerable area with a precise thrust is difficult, at best. Therefore, aim to land a powerful punch in general areas of vulnerability. The face and jaw are good targets. If the situation presents itself, a punch to the solar plexus or groin can be effective. If the attacker's back is to you, the kidney area is a vulnerable spot for a strike. The throat and back of the neck and head are also vulnerable, but strike to these areas with caution because you can cause serious damage.

Until now, we've spoken mostly in terms of punches, and you are probably wondering what's become of the open-hand chop so popular among television and movie producers. To be frank, the chop can be quite effective but it has limited application. It's become widely recognized and associated with karate because Americans initially become enamored with the novel idea of something other than a punch being used in hand-to-hand combat.

But the chop is pretty much limited to situations where your opponent is not able to move away from

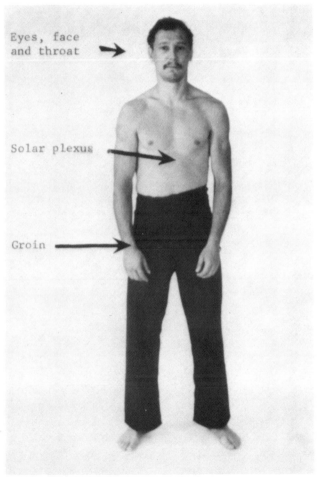

Eyes, face and throat →

Solar plexus ——→

Groin ——→

In a street defense situation, you'll want to strike the areas indicated in this photo and the photo on page 60.

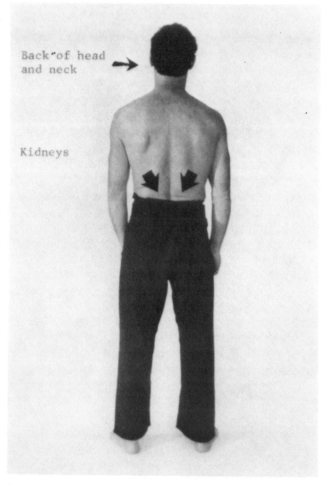

Vulnerable areas of the back, head and neck.

you,rather than in a stand-up fighting situation. Since the chop does generate a great deal of force, it is sometimes used, for example, to disable an arm that you have securely pinned by a holding technique.

Many of the self-defense movements to be shown in this book will, naturally, involve blocking a punch or a kick. We will study many movements which begin with a block, so let's take a moment to study karate's blocking motion. It is important to understand the blocking motion because it will often be the key to your defense.

The theory behind a block is this: one hand will make the initial block . . . the other hand rises and deflects the blow away. This two-handed motion is fluid. Remember, the upper hand makes the initial confact and initially blocks the blow, while the other hand (and arm, too) rises and deflects the blow away, sweeping it away from your body.

The starting position for the upper block. (turn page)

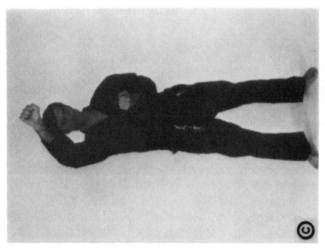

Completion of the upper block, a movement designed to deflect away a blow to your face or upper body. The initial block, shown on the previous page, would stop the blow. The sweeping motion shown here would deflect the blow away.

Note how the middle block accomplishes the same effect with a different positioning of the hands and arms (see below and page 64).

A punch or kick to the lower part of the body calls for a downward blocking movement (page 65 and 66).

Remember that a block, too, will require a concluding act if you manage it (sometimes you simply won't have any option other than to quickly deflect a blow, but you want to follow up whenever possible). As more striking and punching techniques are demonstrated, you'll begin to get an idea of the kinds of responses you might want to use — depending on the situation.

Quite a bit of ground has been covered in this chapter, but there's one more point which is essential to the proper execution of a hand technique—and it is so frequently violated that it deserves special attention.

Starting position of the middle block. (turn page)

The conclusion of the middle block, to block a strike to the middle portion fo your body. It, too, is a fluid motion; make the initial block with one hand, then deflect and sweep the blow away with the other.

The warning is this: Never prolong a hand technique if it doesn't seem to be working. Along the same lines, never chase after a hand or arm as it is being withdrawn. If the hand technique—or any other self defense movement, for that matter—isn't working, *give up on it and try something else.* You will expose yourself to needless injury if you don't.

With that point firmly in mind, let's move on to a method of harnessing tremendous power: executing a proper kick.

Block and deflect a blow to your lower body with the downward block. The initial block would be made with the left hand, as shown above. (turn page)

To conclude the downward block, sweep the other arm across the arm which made the initial block. Remember this is a fluid motion. Don't jerk your arm into three separate positions — flow through it.

Chapter 4

Kicking

Remember the old schoolyard boast of "I could take him with one hand tied behind my back?" Well, it would certainly be a tall order, since the loss of a hand in a fight would eliminate a good portion of your abilities.

But if you think that reacting to a street defense situation with one hand is silly—even suicidal—why would you limit the use of your legs? Electing not to use kicks severely limits your effectiveness, and eliminates one option in your self defense repertoire.

Unfortunately, there is still some reluctance among Americans to defending themselves with a kick. Perhaps there's a long-standing association with the schoolboy concept of a "fair fight," with kicking reserved for girls and sissies.

Today, though, enough exposure has been given to the martial arts that most of us don't automatically associate kicking with dirty fighting. And it's highly unlikely that your attacker will govern his actions by the same code of conduct you would impose on yourself.

The kick is a valuable self defense tool because of the tremendous power your legs can generate. (Try standing or walking on your hands to get an idea of the difference in strength between arms and legs.) In addition, proficiency in kicking gives you another option. When your hands are tied up, all is not lost.

Before we examine basic kicks, a word of warning is in order. In some cases, a shod foot (in layman's terms, a foot with a shoe on it) will legally be considered a deadly weapon. If you do not use discretion while kicking—if, for instance, you have subdued your attacker but continue to kick him senseless—you may find yourself charged with a felony. Likewise, bear in mind that any time you *press* an attack, by chasing after someone, for example, you become the aggressor and you may find yourself in legal hot water. So remember that while you always have the right to defend yourself, don't continue an attack past the point of reason.

With that in mind, let's study the basic types of karate kicks useful in street situations.

The straight front snap kick. This motion may seem a bit unnatural at first, but once mastered it is extremely effective.

The first step is to lift the knee so that the upper leg is roughly parallel to the floor. Holding the toes back, snap the foot forward; remember that you want to make contact with the ball of the foot. Kicking with the ball of the foot helps prevent injury to the toes, which can occur even while wearing a shoe. Keep the ankle pointing straight forward. Always retract any kick with the same velocity with which it was thrown. The reason is simple: If you let the leg dangle in front of you, it is easy to grab.

The straight front snap kick has great range.

After concluding the straight front snap kick — or any kick, for that matter — retract as quickly as possible.

The high kick. This movement is generally used when you are backed into a corner and desperately need room to move around.

Begin the high kick by bringing the knee close to the chest. When you begin practicing this kick, you can carefully use your hands to move the upper leg. With the upper leg almost touching the chest, lash out with the heel. In a self defense situation, you would ideally want to drive the heel into your opponent's chin, face or nose. This is, granted, a very difficult motion, but it has the advantage of surprise. Also, it exposes a minimal amount of your leg to the attacker, making it a useful technique if you are defending against a knife.

The high kick is difficult to master, but it is useful in driving an attacker backward and gaining room for you to maneuver.

The side kick. When executed properly, the side kick
is a good technique to use against a second opponent.
After you have struck the opponent in front of you, you
would snap a kick to the attacker beside you. There are
few set responses to a multiple attacker situation, by
the way, because it is such a varied situation and so
extremely difficult to handle. The best advice for someone confronted by a multiple attacker situation is to
strike decisively at the closest attacker, the one who
appears to be the leader in the attack. Then, a movement such as the side kick will be useful. (Your initial
strike might, of necessity, have to be one of the deadly
force techniques described in **Chapter 7.**)

It's probably wise to limit the use of the side kick
unless you receive professional instruction. If not executed properly, you can injure your hip with this
movement.

Starting position for the side kick.

The side kick can be effective but can also lead to hip injury if not done properly.

The best way to avoid injury is to make sure that you pivot the hip in the direction of the opponent when executing a side kick. When you thrust properly you should feel the heel of the non-striking foot (the foot on the ground) move slightly in the direction of the kick. The side kick makes contact with the edge of your foot and heel.

The back kick is useful when there's little opportunity to escape, or when you are responding quickly to an attack from behind.

Looking back over your shoulder will help properly direct the kick and also help you maintain balance. The back kick is generally executed to the opponent's abdomen. A variation of the back kick which strikes to the knee and shin will be shown in **Chapter 6.**

The back kick. Look over your shoulder when you strike.

Conclusion of the back kick.

The kick to the knee utilizes the edge of the foot. It differs from the side kick because it does not necessarily have to be executed to the side. You can kick the knee effectively if the opponent is in front or to the side of you with this motion.

The kick to the knee is executed with a downward motion, with the edge of the foot driving downward through the opponent's knee. This is particularly effective when your opponent has most of his weight on the leg you are kicking, as shown on pages 76 and 77.

Your first few attempts at throwing practice kicks will surely point out how difficult it can be to keep your balance. That's why practice is essential before you try to use a kick in a street situation.

Be careful when you practice kicking, because legs are very vulnerable to muscle pulls. A good method to practice kicks and develop your balance is to lift your leg, throw a front kick, then—without lowering the leg—throw a side kick and then a back kick. Repeat this series ten times or so without touching the foot to the floor. Then repeat the exercise with your other leg. Gently practice the high kick by working up in height gradually, using your hands to help elevate the thigh.

The kick to the knee. Start . . .

and finish.

When practicing with a partner, don't wear shoes and be careful not to let your kicks land. Kicks pack a surprising amount of power.

The power inherent in a kick means that pinpoint accuracy isn't always necessary. A straight front snap kick can be effective if it lands anywhere on the abdomen. A kick to the groin can be instantly disabling but can be very difficult to land. For one thing, the kick must be aimed at a relatively small area which enjoys natural protection from the legs. Also, a man who is an experienced street fighter will instrinctively protect his groin.

In street situations, kicks below the waist are usually the most useful, although, as mentioned earlier, the high kick has great surprise value and is a good response when you need to gain room. The knees and shins are also attractive targets, by the way, and have the added advantage of immobilizing or slowing down an attacker so you can make an escape.

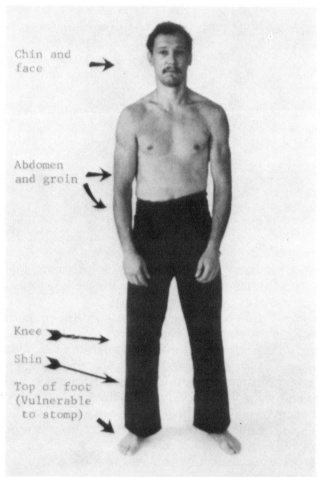

Areas particularly vulnerable to kicks. The chin and face are targets for the high kick, which should be executed only in certain situations.

Kicks can be directed at the head if your opponent is on the ground, but kicking a man while he's down is something that will have to be done on the basis of your own personal code of ethics. There's certainly no easy answer. If your opponent is already disabled, you are morally and legally in the wrong if you kick him while he's on the ground. But if your attacker is armed and angry and able to get up, a kick to the head would be in order.

Kicking is also valuable if you are on the ground. If you've been knocked down and your attacker is hovering above you, the last thing you want to do is try and stagger to your feet. You will be virtually defenseless as you rise.

Instead, position your body so that both legs are facing the attacker. Use your arms to help pivot your body. Kick out with both legs, aiming for your attacker's knees and shins.

Use your hands and elbows to help pivot your body, keep your legs up and kicking. If you've been knocked down, this maneuver will give you time to recover your senses.

When you feel ready to regain your footing, there's a special technique which will let you get up without turning your back on the attacker. Bring your legs up vertically, then move them forward quickly, using their momentum to help you roll forward. Plant your feet firmly and jump up. This is harder than it might appear, and will take a great deal of practice if you are going to use it in a street situation.

There's one other consideration involving kicks. What do you do when someone directs a kick at you? Use essentially the same kind of deflecting motion we learned in the previous chapter. Its application in blocking a kick is demonstrated on page 83 and 84.

Regaining your footing by bringing your legs up, rocking them forward . . .

Until you can plant your feet.

Then, drive upward.

The important factor here is to block the kick with the inside of the wrist, keeping the fingers back to prevent injury. Use the arm to direct the kick away from the body and—if possible—up into the air. As in the photos, the hands can be used to grasp and twist the foot, a movement which is especially effective when the foot is lifted high. If the movement is performed properly, your opponent will wind up on the ground. If the movement does not seem to be working, give up on it and try something else. As we pointed out in the hand technique chapter, it is counter-productive to prolong a movement.

Once again, the deciding factor in who survives a confrontation is often balance. If you can lift your opponent's foot high in the air, he will obviously be off balance and in a weak position. Leverage also plays a key role. By placing yourself in the right position you can exert a virtually irresistible force on the body's weaker joints.

Balance and leverage will be particulary important considerations in the next chapter, which deals with throws and holds.

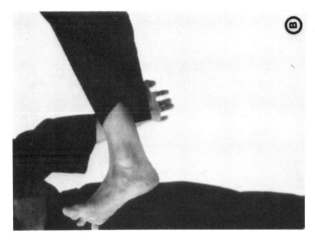

Defending against a kick. Sweep the kick aside, keeping the fingers back as shown in photo B.
(turn page)

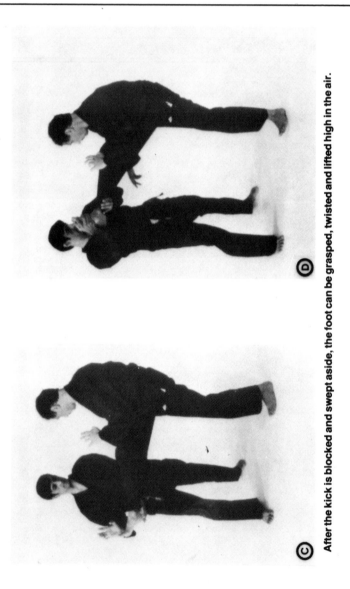

After the kick is blocked and swept aside, the foot can be grasped, twisted and lifted high in the air.

Chapter 5

Throws and Holds

Most throws and holds are directly descended from judo, a Japanese system of wrestling which is more sport that a method of self defense. This is not to say that an advanced student of judo couldn't defend himself; he certainly could, but he would need techniques refined after years of practice.

Throws and holds do have a **place** in self defense, through. They can be used to immobilize an opponent in situations where:

- An opponent is pushing, grabbing and shoving, but doesn't seem inclined to throw a punch. You may not want to escalate the situation by throwing the first blow.
- You are being attacked by a physically inferior opponent and don't want to cause injury. You want to maintain control without using a great deal of force.
- You are legally bound to use restraint. A policeman, peace officer or teacher, for example, generally is ethically and legally limited in the amount of force that can be used in self defense.

If you elect to use a hold, remember that the key to its

effectiveness is not strength, but proper positioning of your body. Twisting an opponent's arm can degenerate into a tugging match if both of you stand toe-to-toe. But when you move to the side and rear of your opponent—using the strength and momentum of your entire body—the force of the hold is greatly magnified.

As an example, let's consider the hand techniques illustrated in Chapter 3. Remember that the preliminary act was deflecting the opponent's attempt to grab you, the technique itself was twisting the hand, and the concluding act was forcing the opponent to the ground.

Suppose you wanted to put a hammerlock-type hold on the attacker. This hold would constitute the concluding act of the movement.

Application of the hammerlock can start from this position. Execution of the hold is shown on the facing page.

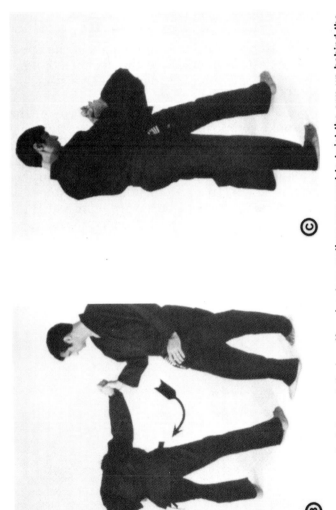

The hammerlock is a relatively self-explanatory motion: you want to twist the arm up behind the back any way you can. Note that the wrist is held with both hands momentarily after the opponent's arm is twisted up behind the back. This gives you the option of breaking away with either hand to hold another part of your opponent's body, as shown in photo D on the following page.

Another useful hold is sometimes referred to as a *shoulder lock,* shown on pages 89 and 90.

You must step forward and to the side of the opponent to engage this hold. Force the opponent's hand and wrist back (this might be done after twisting the wrist in a hand technique).

Using your arm which is closest to the body of the attacker, snake your arm underneath his arm (keeping your grip with the other hand, of course). Grab his wrist and bend the arm back. You may not wish to drive the opponent to the ground with this hold, because he can be effectively immobilized in a standing position because of the bent-backward stance he'll assume to take the pressure off his arm. However, by following through on the hold and taking the opponent down, you can also immobilize him on the ground.

If you foresee the need to immobilize your opponent for a long period of time, you might choose to fall forward on him while maintaining the hold on his arm. Moving the right hand to the elbow increases the holding power of the hammerlock.

The initial block would be made with the left hand, as shown above. (turn page)

Continue to exert more pressure with the shoulder lock. By following through, you can take your opponent down and immobilize him . . .

Most holds are difficult to engage when the attacker is moving. If he is moving rapidly toward you, though, the attacker's own momentum may make a throw the best option.

The type of spectacular throws seen on television are extraordinarily difficult to execute in a street situation. So instead of launching your opponent through the air, be satisfied with simply letting his momentum do him in.

The simple arm throw, for instance, actually involves nothing more than sidestepping an opponent's lunge and guiding him forward, off balance.

If you can manage to get one hand on the wrist of your attacker and one hand on the elbow, the effectiveness of the simple arm throw will be enhanced.

The start of the simple arm throw: side step and grasping the arm. (turn page)

Conclusion of the simple arm throw — throwing the opponent forward.

The reverse take down is useful when you find your-self grappling with your attacker at close quarters.

Both the leg movement and the arm movements must be executed simultaneously in the reverse take down. Extend your arm across the front of your opponent's chest while stepping forward. Step in back of him, placing your leg behind his. Vigorously plant your heel, and at the same time straighten the leg out. The impact of the back of your knee against the back of his knee will begin his fall backwards, along with the pressure of your arm across his chest. Remember, staightening the leg and the push on the chest must be done at the same time.

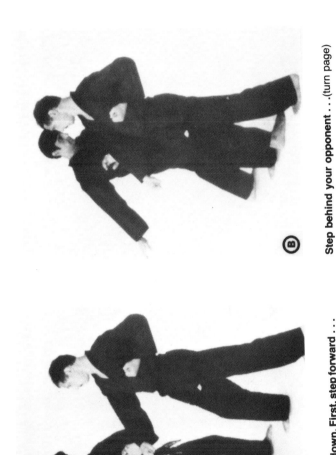

Step behind your opponent . . . (turn page)

The reverse take down. First, step forward . . . .

To complete the reverse takedown.

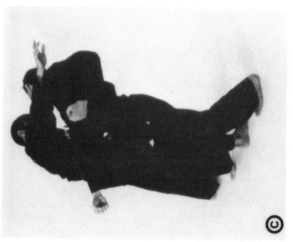

At the same time you step and straighten your leg, use your swinging arm . . .

The next movement, sort of a hybrid between a throw and a hold, is essentially the same motion demonstrated in the hand techniques chapter. But the *arm-block takedown* is such a handy maneuver we want to review it.

The important element here is to get the opponent's arm in a position where the elbow points straight up toward the sky. Keeping the elbow pointed upwards, use your free hand to exert pressure on the elbow, guiding the arm and attacker down to the ground, as shown below.

The last movement to be shown in this chapter is not strictly a hold or throw, but rather an escape technique. It is a *choke break*. Although there are many choke breaks in the martial arts, this one is simple and quite appropriate for a street situation.

The arm-block take down, beginning position. (turn page)

Ⓑ

The arm-block takedown, conclusion.

The twisting motion in this choke break involves turning the body to the side and moving backward; throwing the arm across the body adds leverage to the twisting motion. This choke break appears almost too simple to be effective. Executed properly, this motion (shown on pages 97-99) will break the grip and free your neck.

Only a handful of basic holds and throws have been presented in this chapter, but they comprise an adequate sampling for self defense purposes. Don't forget that holds should be used only when you don't feel that your opponent is really out to do damage. (We're not talking about the choke break, of course, which can be used in any situation.) In other words, you might use a throw or hold to contain your drunken brother-in-law, but don't count on it to be effective against a vicious street attack.

One general guideline to determine whether a throw or hold is likely to be sufficient is the action of your opponent if you take a step backwards during the initial stages of the confrontation, assuming that the confrontation so far has involved verbal abuse and/or some shoving. If, after you step back, the opponent brings his hands up and advances on you, looking as though he is prepared to strike, more severe action than a hold will likely be called for. Unless you are very confident that you can handle your opponent, don't rely strictly on throws and holds for self defense.

You may, though, want to incorporate throws and holds into your overall self defense arsenal. There may come a time when a shoulder lock or a simple arm throw may be the perfect movement, even in a serious situation.

By becoming familiar with a limited number of effective techniques, you have a variety of options while defending yourself. The next chapter will demonstrate how hand techniques, kicks, throws and holds can be integrated and used in actual self defense situations.

(A)

The choke break involves nothing more complicated than . . . (turn page)

And breaks the grip. From this position you can conclude the choke break . . .

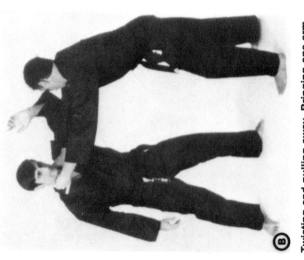

Twisting and pulling away. Bringing one arm across helps accentuate the twisting motion . . .

By smashing back with your elbow.

Chapter 6

Using Hand Techniques, Kicks, Throws and Holds

The biggest problem with most martial arts books is the cookbook approach taken to defense tactics. In other words, "recipes" are provided for a staggering variety of situations. To add to the confusion, the responses are often highly complex and utilize motions which would be difficult for even an advanced karate student.

Let's face facts: An average citizen just won't have the time or inclination to master a wide variety of movements. Unfortunately, however, books with page after page of intricate karate maneuvers seem to have great appeal. Perhaps it's comforting somehow, for people to talk themselves into believing that they have memorized all the material and will be able to instantly call up the perfect recipe.

It just doesn't work that way. For effective self defense, you must become adept at a limited number of techniques and apply them to the situation at hand. You will also have to improvise on the spot. If a technique fails, you must come up with another one—quickly.

If you were to ask an experienced karate teacher what the proper response would be to a punch, he might tell you to "block and punch back, and kick if you get a chance." Disappointed? Many people might be. After all, they expected to hear something like "grab his arm, throw him over your shoulder, and chop him on the back of the neck before he hits the ground."

Common Sense Self Defense is written with the intent of providing you with an effective arsenal, not a spectacular one. And although there certainly is the need for a proper sequence of actions in response to self defense situations, we're most concerned with your ability to use basic punches, hand techniques, kicks, throws and holds quickly and effectively.

You must be prepared to improvise. Cookbook formulas don't work against uncooperative people like attackers. Take note of the fact that boxers—men who make their living in hand-to-hand combat—don't memorize elaborate step-by-step responses. They generally limit their combinations to three punches. They adapt, change their strategy according to the situation. And they use simple blocks and evasive maneuvers to avoid punishment.

They don't always avoid punishment, though, which brings us to an exceptionally important point. Self defense is a give and take situation. You must expect to get hit. To use the boxer analogy again, keep in mind that even the most outclassed pug usually gets in his licks, even if he's fighting the world champion.

This concept is critical. Most citizens—male and female—react with panic when they are hit. Where an experienced fighter might use long, quick punches to keep his opponent away while he clears the cobwebs in his head, a person who hasn't had a fight since grade school is just as likely to cover his head, freeze in fear, and get beaten to a pulp.

As an example, imagine how you would react if you were sitting in a chair and were attacked by someone who throws a punch at your head. By the way, this is a much more common attack than you might think. Would you cover up and hope someone helps you? If you do; you'll wind up in the predicament pictured below.

The correct response is not a cookbook recipe involving an intricate Oriental secret, either. It's nothing more than a block and grab (page 105 and 106).

Because you can't see, you can't react. If you try to rise from this position, you would be extremely vulnerable.

What you've done is to take away the attacker's advantage. When he was standing above you, he was punching down, generating a great deal of power. You, on the other hand, were in a very weak position to fight back.

Now, let's assume that your grabbing technique didn't work well. What's next? As mentioned before, self defense is largely a matter of using all your options. Instead of trying to prolong what's turning into an ineffective technique, immediately try something else: Kick him, driving him back and away.

Take a few moments to analyze what's been presented. What made one course of action—covering up—a total disaster, while the other—even though it took two tries—was a success?

1. The defender using the correct response didn't panic. Holding his head back, but not covering it up, he was able to keep his eyes open, block, and wait for an opportunity. Panic is not easy to control, because people simply aren't used to being attacked. But by developing an alert, self-confident attitude, you can go a long way toward keeping your cool in a dangerous situation.

2. The defender who was successful made a quick effort to bring the attacker down to his level. This was an intelligent response, allowing him to buy time, avoid punishment, and get to his feet.

3. In the next example, we assumed that the grabbing technique didn't work. The defender didn't prolong the technique, but wisely tried something else. He used another set of tools, his feet.

We will now look at some more defenses **common to** street and social attack situations. (Although most of the techniques in this book are directed against what we might term "street criminals," it's important to remember that many attacks also take place in social situations, such as parties, bars, and outings in a city park.) Please note that the techniques about to be demonstrated aren't the only responses, nor will they always be the best responses. They are simply the best bet you'll probably have in these situations. Also, the techniques shown in this chapter are practical applications of the hand techniques, punches, blocks, holds and throws shown so far, along with some additional movements which might prove handy.

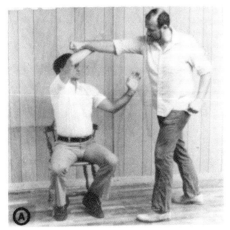

Keeping his eyes open and head up the defender was able to block . . .

And pull the attacker down to his level.
(turn page)

After the attacker has been pulled down, it's safe for the defender to stand up.

Breaking away from a grip. This is a new movement which can be very important. Often, an effective break from a hold can discourage an attacker from pursuing you after you've demonstrated the ease with which you can escape his grip.

This movement is relatively easy once you get the hang of it, and can be practiced with a partner without much risk of injury. This technique involves pushing your wrist against the attacker's thumb, putting pressure on the weak point in your opponent's grip. To do this movement, keep your elbow down, turn your wrist so that the narrowest part of the wrist faces the gap between your attacker's thumb and fingers, and pull away. Don't tug backwards. This motion is difficult to describe, so be sure you practice it with a partner. You'll be able to tell immediately when you are performing the movement properly. (see pages 108-110)

Spinning out of trouble. Many attacks begin with a shove, into an alley perhaps; your attacker wants to get you in a private spot where more punishment can be

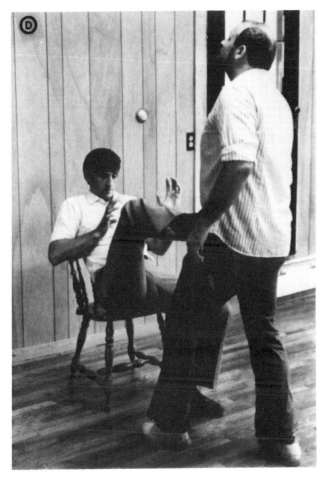

If at first you don't succeed, try again. This time, use a kick.

inflicted in privacy. This technique, also a new one, is very useful, and is pictured on pages 110-111.

You might have to overcome your natural reaction, which is to push back. By spinning, you avoid the thrust of your attacker, use his momentum to put him off balance, and put yourself in a position to strike him.

Getting out of a corner. Use the high kick taught in Chapter 4 and illustrated on page 113.

The high kick is a very difficult motion. But we keep bringing it up because it is extremely effective when you are cornered and need room.

Getting through a doorway or set of stairs. If someone is obviously trying to block your way, there's nothing fancy about the proper response. If you believe that the person blocking your way wants to injure you, and you can't back away, kick him in the gut, as shown on page 112.

Breaking away from a grip. Keep your elbow down . . .

And pull upward. Don't tug backward. Note in photo C . . .

The proper path you want your wrist to take — the narrowest part of your wrist escapes between the gap of your opponent's thumb and fingers. At the conclusion of the grip break . . .(turn page)

Here's the first step in spinning out of trouble. Instead of letting the attacker push you into the parking garage . . .

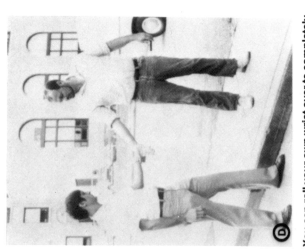

You can roll your own wrist over to completely break the hold.

Ⓒ **And let the attacker's momentum work against him.**

Ⓑ **Sidestep the push . . . .**

Here, a straight front snap kick is used against an opponent who tries to block you from the stairway. Be prepared to move quickly after kicking. As always, retract a kick with the same velocity with which it was thrown. Don't give your opponent a chance to grab it. A possible follow-up shown above, is to pull your doubled-over opponent forward after you've kicked him.

This kick, if you can manage it, will give you room to escape. The high kick is difficult to master but can be very effective.

Use a straight front-snap kick for this movement. You could follow up with a punch if the kick doesn't drive the person back far enough.

Disabling an assailant who attacks from the rear. Kick backwards toward the knee, driving the heel down the shin, scraping as hard as possible. Stomp down with the heel on the top of your assailant's foot.

As you stomp, throw the head back, striking the attacker's face with the back of your head. This will hurt him more than it hurts you. As explained in the photo caption, you can also strike at the groin. Going for the groin might become your only option if a powerful attacker has you lifted off the ground. You can also grab his groin area, squeezing very hard. (see pages 114 and 115)

Escaping a full nelson. It's possible that someone accosting you from the rear could attempt to put you in a full nelson. He might want to hold you in this position while an accomplice works you over.

Push your shoulders down when you feel the full nelson being applied. (Drive your elbows down, in other words.) Then lift your arms and drop down quickly. From this position, you can turn and punch to the groin, as shown on pages 116 and 117.

Fending off an attack from the side. If your shoulder is grabbed, make a full circle with your arm to dislodge the aggressor's grip (see pages 118-119).

After dislodging the grip, your arm will be upraised. You can strike downward with the fist or with a chop. (Use the side of the fist with a hammer-like motion.) You can also stomp your attacker's foot while executing this movement.

Blocking windmill punches. A common type of attack involves an aggressor moving in and raining punches on you. The defense is difficult, but if you throw blocks in rapid succession, the punches can be deflected (see page 120).

By avoiding the initial attacks, you gain time to respond with a punch or kick.

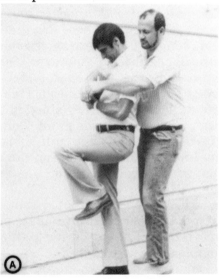

To disable an opponent who attacks from the rear, use your heel . . .

To kick the knee, scrape down the shin, and stomp the foot. You then should drive the back of your head into the attacker's face. Note that when the head moves backward, the groin moves forward. A strike to the groin could be an excellent follow-up from this position.

Drive your elbows down to break the grip . . .

Move quickly when escaping a full nelson . . .

And follow up with a blow to the groin.

It's important to follow up any action with the response you feel is appropriate. Don't stand and watch after you deflect a punch. Wage a continual offense and defense until the situation is resolved.

One way to develop your proficiency is by role playing. Imagine what kind of attack you might be subject to and rehearse your response, both mentally and physically. (This is the tactic Muhammad Ali used to prepare for a fight; he would run through all the contingencies in his mind, over and over.) If you have a partner, carefully role play with him or her and rehearse the types of movements you would use.

Being prepared will aid you in thinking clearly during a stressful situation. This ability is probably the most valuable facet of your defense. Keep in mind that you need the presence of mind to determine how much danger you face, whether you should continue the attack, and how much force to use.

You must respond to the actual level of danger: danger to your health, not your ego. If you truly believe that your life is in danger, deadly force is your next option.

Dealing with an attack from the side. The movement of your arm . . .

will break the grip. Now, you can prepare . . .

A double strike, hitting your attacker on the nose and stomping your heel on his toes or instep.

Throw blocks as quickly as you can when confronted with a toe-to-toe puncher. Look for an opening to follow up by launching your own attack.

Chapter 7

Deadly Force

Deadly force is exactly what the term implies, and in a frank discussion there's no point in being squeamish about what the techniques are designed to accomplish. The intent of this chapter is to demonstrate movements which can maim, cripple or kill.

The tone of this chapter will be quite different from earlier sections of the book. Where moderation and caution were stressed before, these techniques must be executed as viciously as possible—for they are only for use in situations where your life is in danger. When your life is at stake, there is no room for hesitation. These techniques must not be done half-heartedly.

Once again, it must be stressed that the use of deadly force is reserved for predicaments where you are facing serious injury or death. If you use deadly force indiscriminately, you may face civil or criminal action. Even when you feel that the use of deadly force was warranted, be aware that you'll have some explaining to do if you kill the attacker.

To protect yourself from legal hassles[1] and your own pangs of conscience,

- DO NOT use deadly force if you have already turned the tables on your attacker and are attacking or chasing him.
- DO NOT use deadly force when help is imminent—when friends or police are right at hand—unless you truly believe your life is immediately on the line.
- DO NOT use deadly force if you just couldn't live with the results. Many people would rather take their chances than maim or kill someone. There's no reason to be ashamed of this attitude; it's not easy to overcome a lifetime of never injuring another human and suddenly use deadly force. Remember, though, that your attacker won't be playing by these rules.

Now, let's examine some deadly force techniques. We won't pull any punches in the descriptions, and you must not use any restraint in executing these movements if your life is indeed on the line.

Twisting the head starts by grabbing ears and/or hair . . .

1. Remember, laws regarding self-defense vary from state to state.

Putting all your strength into the movement. Use head-twisting only in a life-or-death situation, because, properly done . . . (turn page)

Pull your arms apart violently . . .

It will break your attacker's neck.

Twisting the head. This maneuver is for close-in situations, such as stabbing or rape. (There are some special considerations for defense in a rape which are covered in Chapter 10.) Twisting the head can be used in a desperate situation where you may already have been stabbed or shot and need an instantly disabling tactic before being wounded again.

Place one hand across the attacker's face and place the other hand in back of the head. Grab onto ears or hair. Pull your arms apart violently. Correctly done, this movement will break the attacker's neck.

Thumbs in the eyes. This movement can also be used in close combat situations.

Lock your thumbs as shown in the photo. Remember that the point of this tactic is to disable the assailant, so don't use a light poking motion. Drive your thumbs forward.

Crushing the esophagus. Don't, under any circumstances, practice this maneuver with a partner or even on yourself. It's easier to damage the esophagus than you think.

Into your attacker's eye sockets.

Drive your thumbs . . .

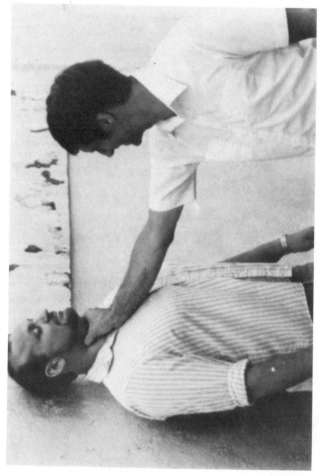

Crushing the esophagus. The sequence in this attack is to grab, crush, and rip.

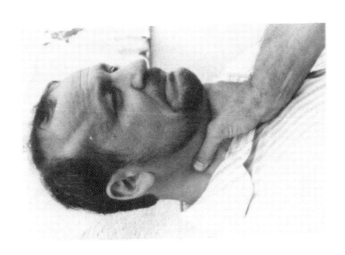

Wrong. Pressure is spread out across the neck because the grip is too wide.

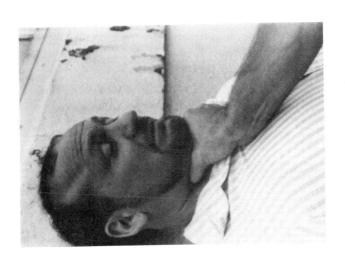

Right. Pressure is on the esophagus.

When you grab the throat, don't place your hand around the neck. Instead, grab for the outline of the windpipe.

Dig your fingers in and grasp the windpipe, which will feel something like a stalk of bamboo. When you have a firm grip, yank toward you. This movement is very likely to kill your attacker.

Note that in a life-or-death situation any blow to the throat—a punch, chop or poke with outstretched fingers—can be fatal.

Chop to the back of the head or neck. If the situation warrants striking to this dangerous area, it warrants using full force.

This movement can be effective when someone has just lunged past you. It will be more effective if you have the attacker somehow immobilized.

Punch to the temple. The same cautions apply to this movement as apply to the chop to the back of the head or neck.

Striking the back of the head or neck can be done either with a chop or with the edge of a fist.

Use knuckles or the side of the fist for a blow to the temple.

The problem with striking to the temple is that a miss by a matter of inches will lead to bouncing a punch off the hard surface of an attacker's skull.

Using Deadly Force Techniques to
Defend Against an Attacker With a Weapon

Television programs and movies have given birth to a dangerous myth: that it's a relatively easy matter for a heroic type to kick a weapon from the hand of an assailant. The truth, though, is that a person attacking with a weapon rarely loses it. And if you think that kicking a knife out of a hand is easy, try hanging a rubber ball from a string, letting it swing and kicking at it. The ball doesn't have a mind of its own, either, so imagine how difficult it will be to kick at a hand that's trying to evade you.

There's no question that the best initial defense against a weapon is a calming technique, which will be discussed in **Chapter 15**. The best defense of all, of course, is keeping away from areas where someone is likely to pull a knife on you.

But when you have absolutely no choice, there are some last-ditch maneuvers for dealing with a weapon. They should be followed up by escape, if feasible, or by a deadly force technique.

Just about all weapons fall into three categories:

Edged and/or pointed weapons. It's possible, but not probable, that you can kick the weapon away. Since the foot generally has a shoe on it, it has some protection.

The crescent kick is named for the shape of the arc it follows. Remember you can't just kick the knife aside and then hope for the best. You must immediately follow up. There are any number of techniques you can use. Just make sure that the response is fast and decisive.

The crescent kick . . .

Follow up is essential. Here, the attacker's arm is grabbed after the knife is kicked aside. The arm can be pulled . . .(turn page)

Follows a short, crescent shaped arc.

It can be twisted behind the attacker's back . . .

After the arm is pulled . . .

And the attack concluded with a chop to the neck.

Another point to consider is the fact that you can block the knife with your arms and hands, as you would a punch. Accept the fact that you are likely to be cut.

After investigating many knife attacks, it has become tragically apparent that the victims instinctively had the right idea but didn't know the procedure. Their hands and arms were often riddled with what coroners call "defense wounds." The victims knew they were being cut, of course, but instinctively tried to protect vital areas with their hands and arms. If they had used the standard blocks shown in Chapter 3 and followed up with a deadly force technique, they might have survived.

Blunt instruments. If you can't run away from a club attack, run *toward* it. Yes, it does seem counter-productive, but keep in mind that the end of the club is going to be the fastest-moving part, the part that will do the most damage. So unless you can get far away, moving back will expose you to more damage.

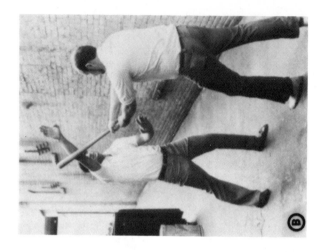

By moving in and blocking, the most forceful part of the blow is avoided . . .

and the club deflected.

Try to block the part of the weapon closest to the attacker's hand, since it will have the least velocity. Let the club slide down your arm, away from your head and body, and follow up with a decisive technique.

Firearms. It's difficult to advise anyone to try to take away a firearm, under any circumstance. Almost any alternative is preferable to moving against an attacker who has a gun. If the gunman is after money, give him all you have. Only if being shot at close range is an unquestionable event should you attempt an attack.

There is a possibility that you could use a fast and hard blocking motion to the side to knock the gun aside. If you do, there must be immediate followup. If your assailant is armed with a revolver, be aware that a grip on the pistol's **cylinder may prevent the cylinder** from rotating and moving a round underneath the hammer. This won't work if the revolver is already cocked. If you don't know the difference between an automatic and a revolver, see **Chapter 8.**

If you are being shot at, your last alternative is to hide behind something. This sounds obvious, but it's likely that you would freeze up in this situation if you haven't given it any advance thought. Police offices are taught to take cover, and to hide behind *anything*. There are cases on record where a police officer has escaped death by ducking behind a fire hydrant or a light pole. The intent was not so much to block the bullet as to throw off the gunman's aim. Most people aren't very good shots to begin with, and their aim is often hampered further by a cheap gun with a short barrel. If you can get behind even a trash can, it can make the difference between life and death. Remember, take cover when you are being shot at, but don't run for cover if a nearby attacker is holding a gun on you.

It's unlikely that you will be confronted with a gun. But as more and more guns filter into the criminal underworld, many Americans are deciding to carry guns of their own. Whether or not to carry a firearm is a difficult decision, and will be explored in the next chapter.

May enable you, to knock the gun aside. Don't try this unless you believe your attacker is ready to shoot. After knocking the gun aside. . . .

A quick, hard blocking motion . . .

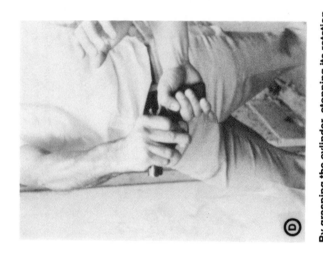

By grasping the cylinder, stopping its rotation (although this won't work with all handguns or with a revolver that has been cocked).

Grab it. If it's a revolver, you may be able to keep it from firing . . .

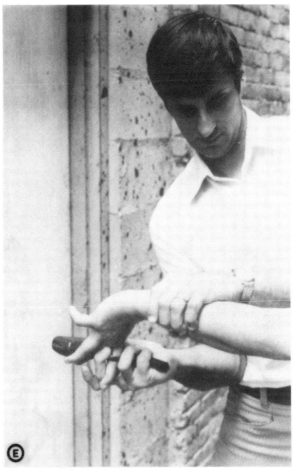

The important consideration here is to keep the gun pointed away from you after knocking it aside. Here, the defender elects to pry the gun from the assailant's hand by bending back the fingers, not tugging.

Chapter 8

Weapons: Firearms

There are two compelling reasons for carrying a gun. They are:

a. Constant exposure to life-threatening situations.
b. Paranoia

Examining your motives for wishing to carry a gun is important. If you actually are in constant danger or have reason to believe that you will be, a handgun may be a reasonable alternative. If paranoia is the motivating factor, you may be asking for trouble.

Why? Because carrying a gun is a hassle. During this chapter, we'll try to give you an honest appraisal of handguns, without moralizing or aligning with any point of view. But there's just no denying that carrying a gun can be more trouble that it's worth.

First of all, even if you are fully licensed to carry the weapon and use it in a situation where shooting was justified, you will enter a legal tangle. Count on spend-

141

ing a few hours being questioned at the police station, seeing your name in the paper, and talking to your lawyer. Maybe that's not the way it should be, but that's the way it is.

Now, what happens if everything isn't in perfect order? If for instance, you don't have a license to carry the weapon, or if there is some question about the justification for the shooting? Expect to explain your case to a judge and probably spend some time in a jail cell. Again, this may not seem fair, but there's no use denying reality.

There are some other factors which may complicate carrying a gun. For one thing, your assailant—who is presumably more adept at violence than you—might pull his gun after you pull yours. Even if he's not armed, the assailant might take your gun away and shoot you with it.

One other problem arises, admittedly a small one, but still worth considering. A gun is something of an albatross to carry around. To keep it concealed, you must wear a coat or sweater, unless you opt for an exotic device such as an ankle holster. A gun is uncomfortable to wear, and if you're at the neighbor's it is generally considered bad manners to take it out and set it on the coffee table when you get tired of having it poke you in the ribs.

Once again, we're not trying to be anti-gun; we just want to point out some of the complexities involved.

If you decide to carry a gun, learn about the weapon and its proper use. (This chapter deals with carrying a gun; the topic of keeping a gun in the house will be examined in Chapter 13.) Join a local gun club; the club will often have guns available for your use before you buy one of your own. By doing some target shooting, you'll be able to appreciate the difference between various gun types.

(Clockwise from top left) .357 Magnum revolver; 9mm automatic; 22 calibre automatic; .38 snub-nose revolver. The .38 has a trigger lock on it to prevent if from being fired accidentally.

Gun talk can get pretty technical, but a few basic facts will serve as a general introduction. First of all, a revolver is named for the revolving **cylinder,** which moves an unfired round beneath the hammer when the trigger is pulled. A double action revolver, the type most practical for self defense, fires with just a pull of the trigger; in other words, you don't have to pull back the hammer with your thumb to cock the weapon, as you would with a single action revolver of the old west type.

For a concealed weapon, short-barreled revolvers such as the **.38 Special** are often favored. This type of revolver is referred to as a snub-nose; the short barrel makes it easier to carry. Convenience has a price, as you'll find if you do some target shooting. The short barrel detracts from the gun's accuracy. Only an expert can handle a snub-nose pistol really well. A novice might not be able to hit a man-size target in a stressful situation at twenty feet. The same applies to small automatics.

A .38 calibre revolver with a slightly longer barrel— four inches—provides greater accuracy but is accordingly more difficult to carry.

A .38 calibre revolver provides a reasonable amount of firepower for most street situations when loaded with standard ammunition. Keep in mind that too much firepower can sometimes be a disadvantage: A screaming bullet can wound innocent bystanders even after punching through a wall or the target.

If you want a high-powered revolver and are willing to lug it around, a **.357 Magnum might be your choice.** It is usually not carried concealed, but a large man can keep it reasonably concealed with a shoulder holster.

Weapons can also be carried on the belt.

Popular holsters are shown on the following three pages.

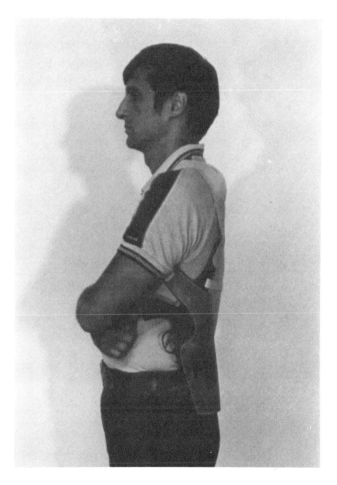

The shoulder holster is a convenient way to carry a pistol. This model holds a .357 Magnum.

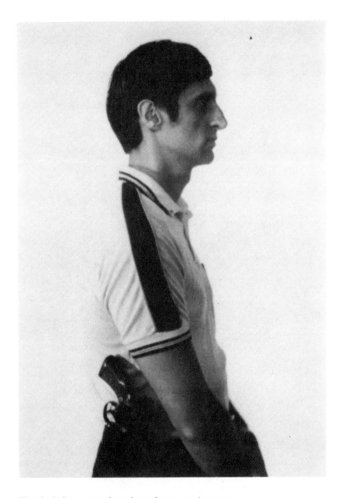

The belt is a popular place for a snub-nose.

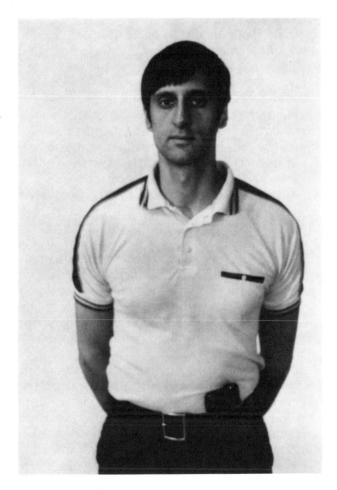

This holster fits inside the belt and holds a .22 calibre automatic.

A very small gun can be carried in a holster which fits inside the belt.

Very small pistols like the .22 automatic can be stuck in a pocket. Remember that they are correspondingly lower in power and may not have the stopping power you desire.

If the ratio of weight vs. firepower is your primary concern, an automatic may be your choice, such as a 9 mm or a .32. These automatics pack quite a wallop. The design of the automatic allows it to use the power of the expanding gases more efficiently. It is also flatter than a revolver and easier to carry in most cases.

An automatic must have a round chambered or a safety disengaged before it is ready to fire. Having a round chambered can be a particular hazard for someone new to handguns, because a bullet stays in the chamber, ready to fire, even after the clip has been removed. An accidental shooting may result from the supposedly "empty" gun. This points up the need for proper training in the use of weapons.

In some localities, training is offered by police departments, and is sometimes required as part of the licensing process.

The licensing process, incidentally, is something you must follow to the letter. In those states which require licensing and/or training, you can wind up in jail for possession of a weapon if you don't follow the rules. Determine who in your community controls the licensing and registration of handguns and follow their procedures exactly. You can locate the proper agency by calling your local police department. If you feel that you are not being given complete information, contact the National Rifle Association for further details.

Be sure to take care of all the loose ends before buying a handgun. It's best to shop at a reputable gun shop, instead of buying from a friend or a friend of a friend. Gunshops almost always stock a good variety of used handguns which can provide high quality at a reasonable price. A reputable dealer will also steer you away from a so-called "Saturday night special," a cheap, poor-quality weapon which is inaccurate and sometimes even dangerous to the user.

If you sincerely feel the need to carry a gun, by all means investigate the avenues open to you. In the event that local laws make carrying a gun impossible— or if you simply decide against it—a less lethal weapon may be more practical.

Chapter 9

Other Personal Defense Weapons

Let's examine a bit of history which will shortly become relevant. During the sixteenth century, invading Samurai warriors took over the island of Okinawa and immediately outlawed all weapons. The natives—mostly poor farmers—developed methods of self defense utilizing common articles. This facet of karate involved use of such implements as the *nunchukui,* sticks tied together which originally were used as a flail to harvest grain.

Today, practitioners of the martial arts utilize these weapons in formal movements, a *kata.* Unfortunately, the criminal element has caught on to the effectiveness of the nunchukui, causing them to be outlawed in many localities.

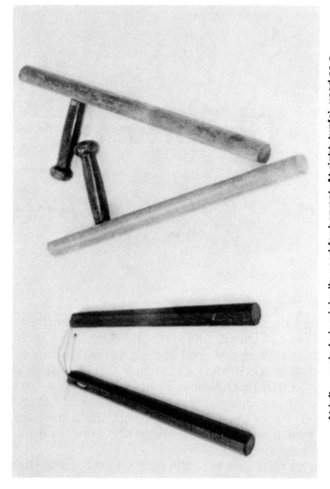

At left, nunchukui, originally used for harvest. At right, tunfai, used as a crank for turning a mill.

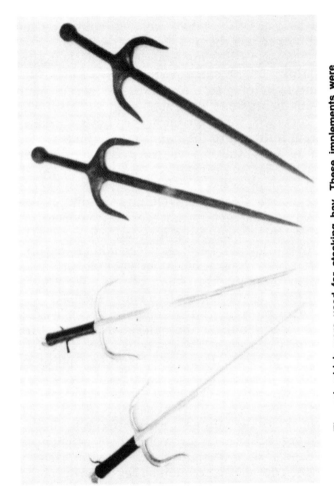

The sai, which were used for stacking hay. These implements were adopted as weapons by the Okinawans, who developed a scientific method of fighting with them.

The point of this history lesson is the fact that when the working class in Okinawa found weapons legislated out of their grasp, they looked around them and created weapons from what was available. And they learned how to use them.

Today, most law-abiding Americans find themselves in something of the same position. Weapons are not commonly available to them. Perhaps there is sound reasonsing behind our laws, such as gun control legislation. However, that legislation has not stopped firearms from falling into the hands of criminals.

But guns aren't the only weapon in the world, and it's essential for anyone concerned with self defense and the defense of his or her family to realize that weapons are everywhere. Just as the Okinawans did, you can find effective weapons in your everyday environment.

Consider the run-of-the-mill pencil. Sharpened and used with precision, it becomes a formidable weapon. It can be driven to the eye, throat, or solar plexus and the region surrounding the solar plexus. We haven't stressed striking to the solar plexus extensively because it can be somewhat difficult to reach with an accurate kick or punch, and is located next to sturdy areas which can absorb a powerful blow. But if the opportunity presents itself, a strike to the solar plexus can paralyze the attacker momentarily. A sharp object, such as a key, can be driven to the solar plexus with excellent effect. Even if it misses the target, it can cause considerable pain as it digs into the flesh.

Don't forget that even an invented weapon can constitute deadly force when directed to a vital area.

A six-inch dowel can accomplish the same purpose as a pencil but it is stronger and more durable. Women, who have available room in their purses, might attach their key ring to a dowel. By holding the dowel, you can swing the keys, using them as a weapon.

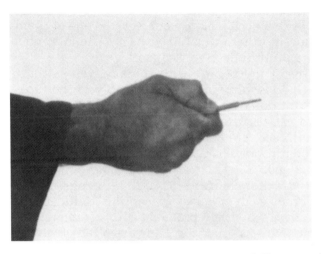

Holding the key firmly in this manner, you can use it to inflict as much damage as a pen knife.

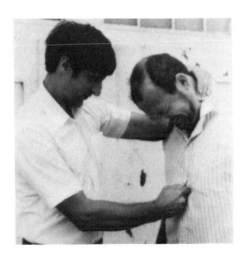

A strike with a pointed object such as a key can cause debilitating pain or injury when directed to a sensitive area. Here it is thrust to the solar plexus. Other targets include the eyes or throat.

Take a good look at your keys. Is one of them longer than the others, and fairly sharp? Then it probably will be a pretty effective weapon.

Instead of poking with the key, you can also use it with a slashing motion, preferably to the face.

You don't necessarily have to improvise a weapon. Pre-packaged self defense weapons, such as tear gas and Mace, are becoming quite popular. This family of preparations irritate the mucous membranes and can be a good deterrent against a sober person. But when an attacker is drunk or high on drugs, his impaired nervous system is less susceptible to its effect.

There's another problem with commercially available tear gas products: They are often of weak concentration and don't contain a powerful-enough propellant. Find out what kinds are available in your community (call the police department or check the local store which sells police gear, which is often an Army-Navy store). Buy some and experiment with it. Don't go so far as to spray yourself in the face, but do take it outside and spray a wall. If you don't feel confident in the particular product, don't carry it. Also, check your local laws to see if you need a license to carry such a product.

Have you ever considered carrying a knife? They are sold in all ranges of sizes and shapes, and have historically been an effective weapon. Knife-fighting is beyond the scope of this book, but you may be able to locate manuals which explain the finer points of this type of combat. Keep an open mind about carrying a knife, but remember that:

- You can wind up in a great deal of trouble if you use a knife against an unarmed opponent.
- You can face weapons charges in the event you are searched during a disturbance in which you were supposedly playing a part.
- You can get into legal hot water if the blade of your knife exceeds local length regulations.
- Like any weapon, the knife can be turned against you if taken away.

This maneuver can be executed in a hurry, and demonstrates that almost any hard or heavy object can be used as a weapon.

Let's return to the subject of improvised weapons. By taking a common object and doing what the Okinawans did, you can have some level of protection without the drawbacks of carrying an obvious weapon. Some improvised weapons can even be attractive. Even a piece of jewelry can suffice.

Take a personal inventory of possesssions which can be turned into weapons. You can probably lay your hands on:

- A rat-tailed comb, which can be used as an effective thrusting weapon.
- A heavy brief case, which can direct a solid blow; you don't have to drop your brief case to respond.

The list of ideas is virtually endless, and you'll be surprised at all the options you can uncover with a little thought.

Another mental exercise involves trying to find weapons in your immediate environment. If you were a pitcher in high school, you might try beaning your attacker with a rock. Ashtrays can be pressed into service in an emergency.

The point is to think on your feet. Use whatever opportunity presents itself. The availability of improvised weapons — and your ability to locate them — will demonstrate that the mind is the most powerful weapon of all.

Chapter 10

Special Defenses for Women

Avoiding Rape

Reading this chapter may leave many disappointed. It could also save their lives.

The disappointment is likely to stem from the fact that we refuse to present the kind of silly, shallow and dangerous advice which seems so prevalent in the media. For example, a newspaper article recently featured a so-called expert who advocated flipping a deck of playing cards in the face of a rapist.

Let's get one thing straight: Dealing with a rapist is not akin to turning aside the advances of an over-eager suitor. A rapist is a violent attacker who may kill you. Don't count on tricks or gimmicks for self protection.

We don't mean to belabor a point, but it's important

to realize that rape is an act of violence, not an act of sexual fulfillment. Since it is a violent act to begin with, it can escalate to greater violence. One recent case we're familiar with began with a woman admitting the attacker, whom she knew, into her apartment. (This is not at all an unusual scenario for a rape; many rapists have known their victims before the crime was committed.) According to court testimony, the attacker, who had been drinking heavily, tied the woman up. During the course of the attempted rape, she struggled and escaped her bonds—only to be stabbed dozens of times. The crime had escalated to murder.

This example is not presented to frighten you, or to imply that most rapists will murder you if you resist. It is intended to point out that the potential for greater violence is always present when you are dealing with a man who is so unglued that he attacks you.

So how do you deal with this type if situation? Avoidance is obviously the best tactic, and we'll discuss it first before moving on to passive and active resistance.

Here are some suggestions for avoiding rape:

- Whenever possible, don't go out alone. Stay with your friends if you go to a bar. Remember that young women who are alone are the rapist's favorite target.
- Avoid being alone with someone you don't know well. Make your first date at a restaurant or movie, rather than your apartment or a picnic in the woods.
- Avoid accepting rides home from men you don't know very well; especially avoid giving rides (or taking them) when a man is drunk.
- By the same token, *you* lose judgement when intoxicated, and may not be able to head off a developing situation or defend yourself. Keep this in mind during social gatherings.
- Park your car as near a building as possible, and park in a well-lighted area. Parking lots are particularly dangerous areas for women, and the situation is aggravated at night. (For your information, most rapes take place between 8 p.m. and 2 a.m.)
- Never admit strangers, remote acquaintances or drunken acquaintances to your home when you are alone.
- Elevators are another source of trouble. If you are suspicious of the person inside the car, take another car or get out of the elevator if the suspicious person enters while you're inside. Always position yourself near the elevator controls.
- Take the home security measures outlined in Chapter 11.

- Keep your windows rolled up and the doors locked when driving. We realize this isn't always possible in hot weather, but if you limit window opening to the driver's side, you can at least roll up the window when you come to a stoplight if you are worried about the neighborhood. Don't leave your purse on the seat in plain view; there's no reason to tempt a criminal to commit any crime. Likewise, don't dangle your purse provocatively when you walk. Purse snatching is a crime particularly troublesome to senior citizens, and will be discussed in depth in Chapter 12.

These suggestions certainly sound simple, even simplistic. There is, of course, no guarantee that following such guidelines will keep you from being raped. But the next time you hear of the rape of someone you know or read an account of a rape in the newspaper, refer back to the above suggestions and see how many of them weren't followed.

Even the world's most sensible woman—whoever that might be—couldn't avoid all dangerous situations. It's just not possible to always travel in groups or avoid being alone with men you don't know well. So if common sense doesn't keep you out of trouble, be prepared to make what could be the most difficult decision of your life.

Should I Resist?

This is purely personal judgement, but you must consider one sensitive point. How important is it to you not to be raped? This might seem like a tasteless and insensitive question, but there's no other way to state it. First of all, keep in mind that resistance frequently results in greater injury to the victim. You may have to face the repulsive choice of determining whether you would rather risk adding to your physical scars or not resisting and risking terrible emotional scars. There is often a sense of guilt—albeit undeserved—on the part of the victim who does not resist.

If you decide to resist, physical action is not necessarily the first option. *Passive resistance* can take various forms. If you can handle it—and the situation allows— it's best to try this strategy before resorting to physical force.

Passive resistance plays on the psychological makeup of the rapist. Although there is no infallible profile of a "typical" rapist, it is generally accepted that most rapists are looking to humiliate weak, terrified victims.

A calm or forceful victim may disrupt the rapist's fantasies to such an extent that the attack will be defused. Use your instincts. You will have to trust your instincts because there is no "right" way to respond to an attack.

If you feel in your gut that this approach may work, and you feel you have the time and gumption to carry it out, you can utilize tactics such as these:

- Prey on his psychological weaknesses. Much of a rapist's problem lies in his inability to relate to women. He may be chronically impotent when normal sex is involved. You might be able to calm him by relating to him, or pretending to relate to him. "I understand how you feel," you could say (even though you don't understand). "You can talk to me." Try to appear as calm as possible.
- Dampen his aggression by not showing fear. Remember, the rapist is likely to be excited by a horrified victim; the more panicky you become, the worse the situation will get. Begging will probably make him more excited. But a calm, unruffled victim is exactly what he doesn't want and doesn't expect. No one is saying that this is going to be easy. You will be pulling the bluff of your life, but your life may be at stake. Try stating in a matter-of-fact, unchallenging tone of voice: "I'm not afraid of you, you know." This may be a good first step toward starting a conversation with the attacker. Use any statement or technique you feel comfortable with; the key is not so much the choice of words but your calm and self confident manner.
- Scream and attract attention. To be frank, in today's society you might scream your head off and get no results. The same applies to whistles and noisemakers. In many cities, a firebarn whistle wouldn't attract attention. (Besides, a whistle might be impossible to reach in an attack, and the rapist could just knock it away.) A whistle might do some good though, but it's best to use it while you're running away, instead of trying to grab it while you're being attacked. If you feel screaming will help—if, for instance, assistance is near—by all means try. Some people suggest screaming "fire!" on the theory that passersby will be more likely to come running to a fire than to a crime. Instead of screaming for help, which might excite the rapist, you might consider screaming at him, loudly, angrily and agressively. The lack of passiveness on your part, combined with the shock value, may disrupt the attack and draw a crowd, too. This strategy does border on being active, rather than passive, defense. It carries the danger of goading the attacker into harming you. It depends on

the situation; you must use your judgement.

- Urinate, vomit, tell the attacker you are menstruating or have a venereal disease. This may or may not be effective, since rape is not based purely on sexual attraction.

If any of these techniques prove successful, run away as soon as you think you can make a successful break. Run toward a group of people and/or a lighted area.

When All Else Fails . . .

Note: This section contains graphic and violent descriptions. Don't be offended. A frank discussion is absolutely essential.

The most important factor in physical resistance is the fact that a weak, perfunctory defense will do little good and could actually do a great deal of harm by angering the attacker. Statistics indicate that the majority of physical injuries associated with rape are minor; by resisting, you do escalate the situation and run the risk of greater injury.

But if you decide that physical defense is what you want to try, your attack must be quick and violent, with *sincere intent to cause injury*. Should you decide to take the risk of defending yourself, always bear in mind that the man is a criminal and you have the right to mount a defense.

Any of the deadly force techniques demonstrated in Chapter 7 are applicable to a rape defense, but since women generally aren't as strong as their male attackers, the responses should be chosen from the movements which require the least amount of strength and grappling.

The eyes are a good target, especially when you drive at them with a sharp object, such as a key. Keep your keys in your hand when approaching your car.

Incidentally, many rape situations unfold as a woman enters a car. Rapists are often attracted to the locale because they want to eventually use the car as a method of escape. So when you approach your car, don't stare blankly ahead. Be alert and gaze in back of the car, and look through the rear window into the back seat.

If you are grabbed, the wisdom of keeping your keys in your hand will become apparent. Even if you can't reach a vital area, the keys can be used to break a grip.

The force of the key strike is magnified if you hold in the firm grip shown earlier.

The throat may become exposed during a rape attack. If you feel you can manage it, go for the throat with your hands (see Chapter 7), pencil or key.

If the attack originates from the rear with a grab to your body, try the kicking and stomping motion shown on pages 168 and 169.

The strike to the groin will be more effective if you use it in combination with the movement of the back of your head into his face. As the face moves back, the groin moves forward.

When the rape is imminent or underway, the man's sex organs are exposed and therefore more vulnerable. If you still want to continue your physical defense at this point, grab the penis and testicles at the base, close to your attacker's pelvis. Hold the testicles somewhat in the manner you would hold a bunch of grapes. Use a violent, squeezing, twisting and pulling motion. Don't be squeamish about this. Put every ounce of strength behind the grip, twist and pull.

Granted, this is an unpleasant scenario. That's why prevention is so important, why it's critical to learn to use your head to protect your body.

Approach your car cautiously, and keep alert. Look through the back window into the back seat.

This woman is in a pretty bad position—her head is pulled back, making it almost impossible for her to strike with hands or feet. But she thinks quickly and jams the point of her key into the back of the attacker's hand. This is very painful.

Hold the key firmly between thumb and fingers to prevent it from falling out of your hand or shifting position.

Stab your attacker in the throat with your key.

To fend off an attack from the rear, start at the knee . . .

and stomp downwards. There's no magic about this movement—it has to be forceful to do damage. After stomping, throw back your head into his face and strike to the groin.

Chapter 11

Special Defenses for Children

Throughout this book we've tried to shy away from oversimplification. Even though there's very little in human behavior that can be taken as a constant, this is as close as you will come:

You can greatly increase the safety of your children by instructing them never to go anywhere with anyone unless you—the parents—have prearranged it and informed your children. Don't ever be inconsistent about this.

Consistency is the key; it's your job as a parent to protect your children, and the whole process will be thrown out of whack if you don't always adhere to the rules you set for them.

For example, let's say you tell your son in no uncertain terms never to accept a ride with anyone, even if he knows that person. (Unless, of course, you prearrange the pickup.) Let's also assume that one day you encounter a personal emergency and send the next-door neighbor to pick up the child—without making a prior arrangement and informing the child.

Regardless of whether or not your child accepts the ride, you have broken your own rule. Your children, who can't cope well with inconsistency, will become confused and less apt to follow your rules in the future. They will also become more likely to be victimized.

Attackers who prey on children—child molesters, kidnappers and the like—will do their damndest to try to make your child violate the rule stated at the outset of this chapter. Police investigations show that the ploy to lure children into a car is often something like, "Your mother is in the hospital and she wants me to pick you up." It will take a strong-minded child to resist that ploy, but your child will be able to *if* you relate these rules to the child. Let the child know that he or she should not accept the ride, but return to the school building (which is probably where the ride will be offered) and tell the principal or other responsible official what is happening. The principal can then handle the situation.

Children really have no physical defense except for running away. That's why it is essential that you spell out some basic safety rules for them.

- Instruct your children never to go anywhere with anyone unless you—the parent—have arranged it and informed your children. It bears repeating.
- If anyone offers to give your child a ride after school—even if it is a family friend—your child should refuse the ride, go back into the school and tell the principal. The principal can arrange for the child to call home. Friends of the family can and do molest children, so just because your child knows the person does not guarantee the child's safety. It may be unlikely but it *can* happen.
- Teach the child to avoid extended or abnormal contact. It's not always an easy distinction to make, but you must set some guidelines. Sitting on a visitor's lap for a minute or two is not abnormal, but long periods could be. While a peck on the cheek is all right, a kiss on a child's lips is not. The purpose of this is not necessarily to steer the child away from that particular person, but to *avoid letting the child develop the habit of accepting such contact from strangers or acquaintances.* The child really can't be expected to

make the distinction among good and bad people (even psychiatrists don't have much luck at that). The habit, then, must be applied consistently. This may anger some relatives, but that's a small price to pay.

- Children should play with others of their own age group. If an adult approaches, children should know not to include him in their play. Child molesters are often childlike themselves and feel they can only relate to children. Your child should be instructed to say something like "I'm sorry, but my parents have told me not to talk to strangers." This shouldn't offend anyone except an extremely ignorant person or one who has evil intentions to begin with. Your child's statement, in fact, will be a sign of good upbringing.

- If someone begins active sexual harassment, your child must get away and stay away. When a person in a car slows down and begins talking to children through the car window—whether he is harassing them or trying to lure them into the car—the best strategy is for them to *carefully* walk in back of the car and cross the street. This will prevent the driver from following them with the vehicle.

Children should cross the street in back of the car if they are being sexually harassed.

Instruct them not to run across the street and to use extreme caution. The traffic is a hazard, too.

- If someone is trying to coerce your son or daughter to go anywhere with him, the child should approach a group of adults, tell them the situation, and stay with them until the danger is past. The next resort is for the child to go to any house and ring the doorbell.
- Movie theaters are favorite haunts for molesters. If someone touches your child or otherwise harasses him or her, the child should be instructed to get up and leave the seat. The child might say something like, "Here comes Daddy" while leaving the seat. It's best for the child to report this to the usher or theater manager.
- Public shopping malls are favorite haunts of deviants, essentially because there are so many unattended children there. The simplest way to combat this danger is not to leave young children alone in a mall, and not to let them visit the bathrooms unescorted. Public bathrooms pose a particular danger. You should escort your children, or at the very least, work out some kind of system whereby they know you will be coming for them if they do not return in a specified period of time. It's generally safer for children to visit the rest rooms together, or, for that matter, to stay in groups everywhere. A single child is a molester's favorite target.
- If the child is abducted, it is essential that he or she know that escape is possible. (This may sound obvious to you, but it is not to the child.) Many abductions have involved a kidnapper taking a child to restaurants, gas stations and motels—without the child understanding the possibility of escape. Make sure your children know that if they are taken to a restaurant they should grab the hand of someone who works there—an employee, not a customer—and ask for help. Also, tell the child that there are police everywhere, not just on the block or in town. Children abducted to a strange place often don't comprehend this fact, or the fact that

173

there are people everywhere who can help in emergency situations.

To summarize, the best defense for children is to learn common sense rules from parents, and for the parents to be consistent about these rules. It would be a terrible shame if you were to violate one of your own rules on this—by sending a neighbor to pick up the child without prior arrangement—because you would be opening the door to trouble.

When you teach these rules to your children, try to let them know that the rules are standard operating procedure, simply a normal routine and not a method of retreating into fear. If you put your child in constant fear, you're going to wind up with a neurotic child. Teaching safety and good habits is the issue here—not trying to scare the wits out of your children by teaching them to distrust everyone and everything.

Chapter 12

Special Defenses for Senior Citizens

This chapter is relatively short because there are very few defenses which apply specifically to senior citizens. For one thing, a healthy man just entering retirement can be just as strong and vigorous as anyone, and can use any of the tactics in this book. On the other hand, a frail senior citizen simply won't be able to manage much in the way of physical defense.

Prevention is always the best option. All the techniques of prevention listed elsewhere in this book (especially home security) are applicable to senior citizens. In addition, here are some which apply more directly to members of this age group:

- Try to do your shopping in the morning, which statistically is a safer time to be out on the street. Travel in groups if at all possible.

- Don't carry a great deal of money. Many older persons have developed the habit of carrying large amounts of cash; this habit was born in much safer days. If you are carrying a roll of money, you not only stand the chance of losing it, but you also can make yourself a repeat target. A mugger who gets $200 from you is likely to keep his eye out for your next trip down the street. Also, you should use a checking account and have your social security checks deposited directly to the bank.
- Women should avoid carrying a purse if at all possible. Senior citizens are particulary vulnerable to purse snatchers, although woment of any age must take precautions. Try carrying your money in a wallet, or in some other container which can be concealed in a pocket. Take only what cash you need. If you simply can't get along without a purse, don't carry it at your side hanging from the strap. This will make things easy and tempting for a thief. Instead, hold the purse close to your body. Don't resist if someone tries to snatch your purse. You may, however, want to try dumping the contents onto the ground. Incidentally, some parts of the country are experiencing a trend of purses being taken out of unattended shopping carts.
- If you must carry a purse, be sure to keep your house key in a separate pocket; you don't want the same person who has your address (from credit or ID cards) to have your house key.
- Sit down on the ground if you are accosted by a purse snatcher; you stand a better chance of avoiding injury this way. Try to get a good description of your attacker—his clothes, his race, the color of his hair, any unusual or distinctive features about him.
- Use a whistle or noisemaker if you feel more secure with it, but don't count on this measure to be infallible.

The elderly are, of course, targets for other crimes than purse snatching. However, it's important to note that except for a few crimes such as purse snatching, the elderly aren't victimized at a higher rate than the general populace. This is important to remember, because if you are seized with paranoia you will probably be a more attractive target.

If you are robbed at knifepoint or gunpoint, it is even more important not to resist the robber. The New York City Police Department points out that it gives the same advice to elderly ladies as it gives to 250-pound weightlifters: When someone pulls a weapon on you, hand over the money.

An assailant who is intent on doing you bodily harm poses a difficult problem. You may not have the strength to mount a physical defense, depending on your health.

If you are relatively young and in excellent shape, you might be able to utilize some of the techniques in this book. Don't forget, though, that your resistance may escalate the situation.

If you feel that some sort of resistance is in order, consider the gentle type of escape maneuvers that are part of *akido,* a martial art which stresses using an opponent's momentum against him.

The spinning out of danger technique described in Chapter 6 is a reasonable option for a healthy senior citizen who wants to avoid being pushed. Since you are probably less agile than you used to be, you'll do less spinning and more stepping, but the principle is the same. If you are pushed, don't push back. Move to the side.

Don't meet a push with a shove. Instead, avoid your opponent's rush . . .(turn page)

**Let his momentum work against him. This maneuver may give you the
split second you need to call for help or otherwise escape the situation.**

There may be times when you need to break free of a
grip. Once again, don't bow to the natural reaction of
starting a tugging match with the assailant; he will
almost always be stronger than you. Instead, use the
standard technique for breaking a grip we showed earlier. A review is on the facing page.

For most seniors, this is about the highest level of
resistance you will want to mount, unless—as mentioned earlier—you are relatively young and in out-
standing physical condition. Your strategy in an attack, first and foremost, is to try to keep from being
injured.

In response to the question that is undoubtedly on
your mind, we do not recommend that a senior citizen
carry a weapon. It's too easy for a faster and stronger
opponent to take it away from you.

Instead, rely on your many years of accumulated
wisdom to steer you clear of trouble.

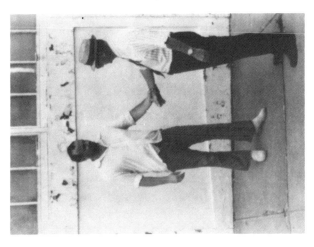

The proper way to escape a grip is by moving your wrist against the opponent's thumb. The movement is described in detail in Chapter 6. Remember not to tug backwards. Keep the elbow down.

Chapter 13

Protection in the Home

- Someone you've never seen before appears at your door, claiming that he called earlier and was told to come over at six o'clock. "Nonsense," you tell him. "My wife and I were both at work all day, so no one here could have told you that." You return to dinner, smugly unaware that you may have just given precise instructions to a thief, telling him when to return and clean you out.
- A man who says he's a salesman seems unusually curious about your belongings. He takes the liberty of walking into another room, complimenting you on your collection of antiques. Justly proud, you elaborate—without stopping to think that you're taking him on a guided tour and giving him an inventory of the property that's worth stealing.
- Across the street, a man with an attache case is going from door to door. A car slowly follows him down the street. He ducks into your neighbor's side yard. You're tempted to call the police, but don't. "It's none of my business," you think.

Although most home break-ins are hit and run affairs, housebreakers may use a variety of techniques to set up the groundwork for an entry, or cover their tracks if caught in the act. Defense of your home, much like street defense of your personal safety, relies as much on the brain as on the body. This chapter will help you to learn when your suspicions should be aroused, and will give you an idea of how to bolster your home security (which will also increase your personal safety and the safety of your family). First, we will focus on some of the physical security measures you can take.

Mountains of books and articles have been written about home security, and there's really nothing new to be added in the way of technical advice. What needs to be stressed is the need for simple, common sense precautions and a healthy awareness of what factors contribute to making a home an attractive target for a burglar.

Note that we said *burglar*. Although prevention of property crime really doesn't come under the strict purview of self defense, we are including a comprehensive section on home security. There are good reasons:

- A burglar can hurt you, although he is more likely not to. In rare circumstances, an intruder may be breaking into your home with the sole intention of harming you.
- Self defense and self confidence in all situations are enhanced by peace of mind—something you can't have if you are constantly worried about your house being broken into.
- Once a home or a neighborhood becomes known as an easy target, criminals are attracted to it. This, of course, will add to the physical danger encountered by residents of the area.

Burglary is one crime which you truly are likely to encounter. It's the nation's fastest-growing felony. It is also one of the most preventable of crimes, if homeowners and apartment dwellers take the proper precautions.

"Taking the proper precautions" sounds a bit obvious, doesn't it? Apparently, it hasn't been made obvious enough, because crime statistics show that 40 percent of burglaries take place via an unlocked door or window. As police are quick to point out, a lock doesn't lock anything until *you* lock it.

Not to belabor the issue, but it's very important for

you to bear in mind that home security doesn't necessarily have to involve such elaborate precautions as alarm systems or guard dogs. Simply making sure that your locks are engaged can make a difference. Granted, it won't keep out someone who really wants to break in, but when you consider that most burglars are amateurs following the path of least resistance, it makes sense to tip the odds in your favor.

So before we look into the more expensive and intricate alternatives, let's examine the simple approach. Please don't skip over this section because you think that the material is too obvious to be worth your while. These measures *are* effective, and when dealing with a burglar—who really doesn't want to encounter a lot of trouble while breaking in—anything you can do might be the deciding factor.

First, you'll have to start thinking like a criminal. If you were a burglar, how would you break into your own house? It's admittedly an odd question, but asking it— and trying to find the solution—might, in the long run, save you money, frustration and heartache.

By a little constructive role-playing, you can uncover the weak spots in your home security, the same weak spots that a burglar could exploit. And through some common-sense, relatively inexpensive measures, you can shore up those problem areas.

Ready? Grab a notebook and start in the yard. If you were a burglar, see if you could:

- See into the house and take an inventory of everything of value. Try this at twilight with the drapes open and you might be shocked. When the lights are on, it's virtually like putting your possessions on stage. An open garage door is also inviting. There's a lot of valuable property in most garages, and a cruising thief just might make a mental note to stop back for the bicycles, tools and snowtires he's seen on display.
- Find a spot near a door or window where you are completely hidden from view. If you can find such a location, don't be surprised if a burglar can, too. A cozy hiding spot behind a large shrub, for instance, could provide a burglar with an extended period of time to work on a lock.

Can you see anything worth stealing in this garage? So can a cruising thief.

- Take a door off its hinges. Yes, some exterior doors do have the hinges facing out, and if the lock proves to be a problem, an enterprising burglar might just pull the hinge pins and remove the whole door.

By now, you've probably got the idea, and a more detailed inspection may turn up some other chinks in your armor. In many cities and towns, the local police department will have a crime prevention unit which will send out an officer to do a security survey. Take advantage of this service if it is offered. It's usually free (at least it costs no more than you've already paid in tax dollars).

How do you deal with the problem areas you've uncovered? Often, the best course of action is relatively inexpensive and based on simple good judgement. The shrubs which obscure a basement window, for instance, might have to undergo an enthusiastic session with the hedge clippers. Drawing the drapes in the evening will enhance your privacy and screen greedy eyes, as will habitually closing the garage door. And even the unhandiest of handymen can take a stab at reversing the door hinges.

Here are some more simple methods to improve the security of your home:

- Install good locks. Yes, it's been said before, but as one veteran cop pointed out, "You just wouldn't believe the Mickey Mouse things people have on their doors." Good-quality deadbolt locks are a deterrent, and don't have to cost a fortune, especially if you are able to install them yourself. Even if you have to call a locksmith, the bill for five locks can, in some parts of the country, be under $250. Detailed information on locks will be presented later in this chapter.
- Pin your windows. Drill a hole where the sashes meet and insert a nail; another option is to buy commercially available screws specifically designed for this purpose. You can pull out the nail or draw back the screw when you want the window open, but when the window is pinned shut it will be very difficult to open from the outside—certainly more difficult to force open that if it's only secured with the "clamshell" type lock found on most windows.
- Keep your property line well-maintained. Fences and hedges are more than just a physical barrier: They are a psychological restraint. Well-kept hedges or shrubs leading to your front door, for instance, will discourage someone from stepping over them and wandering around to the side of the house. He will look out of place and feel out of place. A thorny hedge on the yard side of the fence will make an unattractive landing-place for someone who is considering hopping the fence.

This commercially made window-locking screw holds the sashes together, and it turns only with a form-fitting tool, which is sold along with the screws. This type of device is a good option for when you go away on vacation; if you choose to lock windows in this manner when you are home, remember that you could be locked in if a fire erupts, so keep the special tool handy.

- Keep your residence looking like it's occupied whenever you are away. Mechanical timers can be bought cheaply; they turn lights on and off at specified times. A radio playing can also help. By the same token, don't leave clues that you're not home, such as piled-up newspapers or unshoveled snow. Never leave a note on the door saying that you will return shortly.

- Install good outside lighting. As far as burglars are concerned, the less light the better. Important: Have the outside lighting controled by a switch indoors. If you hear a noise, you can check out the yard by looking out the the window and flicking on the switch—without placing yourself in danger.

- Get to know your neighbors and encourage them to keep an eye on your property. In return, of course, you must keep an eye on theirs. The neighbor who thinks an intruder cutting through another yard is "none of his business" just might be next on the list himself. Collective security is probably the most effective measure you can undertake, if you can generate cooperation. Police officials are almost unanimous in their contention that the eyes and ears of a concerned public are the most efficient law enforcement tools at their disposal.

Such simple measures as these admittedly aren't a cure-all; if you have items of great value or other compelling problems, perhaps an alarm system is needed, along with more elaborate physical security precautions. Remember, though, that even though no security measure is foolproof, doing something is better than doing nothing.

Consider good locks first. The lock situation is a good example of a measure so basic that people often ignore it. In fact, a surprising number of people—people who really should know better—don't have the faintest notion of what a deadbolt is and why it's an effective device.

The easiest way to explain it is that a deadbolt is a lock which engages only with the turn of a key or a thumbturn device. You can tell if the lock on your door is a deadbolt by opening the door, throwing the lock, and pushing on the bolt—the piece of metal that projects out from the door. If the bolt retracts, you don't have a deadbolt.

The theory behind a deadbolt is this: the "spring-latch" type of lock commonly found on a front door is designed to snap closed as you shut the door behind you on the way out. But the wedge-shaped bolt which retracts as you shut the door and springs back into place *can also be pushed back with any device which fits* between the door and the jamb. This weakness has led to the police officer's nickname for the device of a "credit card lock."

Statistics show that many entries are made by forcing an inadequate lock, such as the so-called "credit card lock." If you make it hard for a burglar, by having a good lock, he'll be tempted to look for an easier target. There's a school of thought that says, "If they want to break in, they will, so why bother?" This theory doesn't take into account that most break-ins are committed by amateurs, and amateurs can be deterred if they run

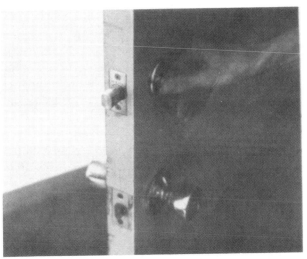

The top lock is a deadbolt. The lock on the bottom is a spring-latch type, wedge shaped and designed to snap shut as you close the door behind you. If you want to add a deadbolt, it can simply be installed above your present spring-latch lock, as it was in this case.

into difficulty. Remember, we're talking mainly about hit-and-run types when we speak about a typical burglar, not a professional with a pocketful of lock picks. That's why most security advisers recommend a deadbolt lock with at least a one inch throw.

A "throw" refers to the length of the bolt which will extend into the receiving hole in the door jamb. Since the deadbolt only retracts when the lock is turned with a key or thumbturn, it is less susceptible to prying with a credit card or screwdriver. And since it has a longer "throw" than a typical spring-latch bolt, it's less likely that an intruder will be able to force the door frame far enough apart to disengage the bolt from the door jamb.

There are two basic types of deadbolt locks, a single cylinder and a double cylinder. (The cylinder is the part of the lock which accepts the key.) A single cylinder lock operates with a key from the outside of the door and a thumbturn from the inside. A double cylinder lock is just what the name implies: it has two cylinders—one on each side of the lock—and must be operated with a key from the inside and outside of the house. The advantage of a double cylinder lock is that it can't be opened by a burglar who breaks a pane of glass and reaches in.

A double-cylinder lock is generally used when there is glass within 36 inches of the door (an arm's reach). But some homeowners opt to replace glass in or near a door with an unbreakable plastic instead of installing double cylinder deadbolts. Why? Because a double cylinder lock can also lock you *in,* and in a fire, for instance, it may not be easy to locate the key to let yourself out. So if you decide to install double-cylinder deadbolts, you should either leave the key in the lock when you're home (on the inside, of course) or have it located in a nearby spot where you can lay your hands on it quickly.

A side view of a single cylinder deadbolt.

A side view of a double cylinder deadbolt.

How do you go about installing deadbolt locks? Someone who is handy with tools can do the job; installation instructions generally come with the locks. The best kind of lock is one that is morticed into the door, which involves using a drill or a hole saw. You can call a locksmith if you don't feel up to the task.

Count on spending about $20 to $40 apiece for a residential lock of reasonable quality (double cylinder locks will be at the higher end of that range) but be prepared to encounter widely varying prices. The differential may result from the quality of the lock itself, the cost of living in your area of the country, or services offered along with the sale. Some locksmiths, for example, will include in the purchase price changing the cylinder to accommodate your present house key.

If you decide to make the investment, shop around. Compare the best buys, taking into account the service offered before and after the sale.

If you have a good deal of valuable property or live in a high-crime area, you may wish to spend more money on more elaborate precautions. An old joke holds true in this case: The perfect gift for the person who has everything had better be a burglar alarm.

An alarm can protect you by sending out a silent signal to the alarm company or police headquarters, or by sounding a noisy bell or siren. Silent alarms, however, are more common in commercial establishments, because the primary emphasis in home security is usually scaring away the intruder, rather than catching him in the act.

Alarm mechanisms work in a variety of ways. One of the most common methods of operation is via magnetic switches placed on doors and windows. The switches don't usually touch, but they keep the circuit closed when they are within a very small distance of each other. When the circuit is broken, an alarm sounds.

These systems can be installed by a do-it-yourselfer, but involve stringing wires from place to place. A handy homeowner can figure out ways to run the wires within the walls, but an apartment dweller may have to put up with the wires, unless his landlord will allow him to drill holes in the walls. If you are not skilled in such work, this type of system can turn out to be more trouble that it's worth, although you won't have wasted a fortune. Do-it-yourself packages can be found for under $100.

Also inexpensive are the portable alarms which can be hooked to doors or windows. They give off a noise when motion sets them off. These might be handy for travel, but keep in mind that it might not make enough noise to scare away a burglar, who could step on it or pitch it into the bushes.

A motion detector is another type of alarm which doesn't require extensive wiring. The device sends out a high frequency sound pattern which monitors any change caused by the motion of an intruder. These will be more expensive than the magnetic switch type of alarm system, in many cases because you'll need more than one unit to cover another room. (A magnetic switch alarm system can be expanded simply by adding more switches and wire.) Owners of the least expensive type of motion detectors have occasionally noted that the devices give off frequent false alarms. Pets roaming around the house will set off motion detectors, too.

There are other alarm systems which operate by sensing body heat, or by detecting an intruder with a photo-electric beam. These types, too, can be effective, depending on the quality of the unit and the abilities of the person who installs and plans the system.

There's no question that the best burglar alarm is a system installed and monitored by professionals. Pros might use a variety of alarm mechanisms, tailoring the choice to your individual needs. But a professional alarm system doesn't come cheaply: An apartment system might cost from $500 to $1000, with prices for a house running upwards of $1000.

Incidentally, police are quick to point out that you should buy your alarm system from a reputable firm. If you don't check into the background of the firm installing the system, you may wind up with a company that's gone out of business and a "white elephant" alarm which no one wants to service.

When discussing price with an alarm company, take into account the services offered. If you are hooked up to a central dispatching station, where alarms are monitored 24 hours a day, the alarm company will charge an additional monthly fee plus a one-time hookup fee, which might be in the neighborhood of $200.

Only you can decide if the alarm is worth it. Peace of mind, perhaps, is the most important product of a burglar alarm company. Aside from protection against burglars, some systems will also detect fire.

In any event, an alarm is never a substitute for brains and caution. At the beginning of this chapter, we mentioned the importance of using your head to prevent burglaries. Some examples were given of how a burglar might set a trap for you: tricking you into telling him what your working hours are, or getting you to give him a tour of the house. It is your responsibility to make sure that you or anyone in your family is aware enough not to give out information to strangers. Whenever the questions posed by a stranger get too personal, your antennae should start to tingle.

You can also help to keep a lid on burglary by engraving your property and displaying a sticker warning that your property has been marked. Although a burglar could go to the trouble of grinding off the identification numbers, he probably won't want to. If you have antiques or collectibles which can't be engraved, record any distinguishing marks on them and take photos. This will aid in reclaiming your property should police recover it.

Don't disregard the safety of your neighbor's house. As mentioned earlier, collective security is important because it can result in burglars being caught and it can also result in your neighborhood gaining a reputation as a tough place to get away with a crime. If you see something suspicious, report it. Don't ever waste time in reporting a crime, because a trail grows cold very quickly.

To summarize, your alertness is important in keeping your neighborhood from becoming a favored target for thieves; you can also reduce the threat of a home break in by using simple, common-sense precautions after surveying the weak spots in your home security. One point remains to be considered: What do you do if an intruder enters your **home?**

Statistics indicate that most intruders aren't armed when they break into a home. One factor in this may be the more severe penalties for breaking in while armed. However, there is nothing to stop a burglar from making a trip to your kitchen to pick up a carving knife. Still, though, a burglar is usually interested in stealing your property, not in harming you. That's why burglars like to break into empty houses. If they hear a noise, they will probably run like hell.

But not all will. Don't ever assume that someone who has broken into your home is a harmless and misunderstood victim of society. Defending yourself opens up a controversial and difficult question.

Should you have a gun in the house? Well, there's a catch-22 involved in this issue. Without a gun, you may be defenseless in the unlikely—but possible—event that an intruder tries to harm you. With a gun, you may be endangering the children in your family and may even be indirectly contributing to the crime rate, since many black market guns are obtained during home burglaries.

Your individual situation and judgement must determine whether or not you keep a gun in the house. We can't make recommendations on what is a personal decision, but we can tell you something about home weapons.

First of all, a home pistol doesn't have to be the snubnose type, because it doesn't have to be carried or concealed. A .38 calibre pistol with a four-inch barrel (rather than the snub-nose) is a good choice for a home defense weapon. It is large enough to provide power and reasonable accuracy, it is easy to learn to use properly, and it doesn't send out an extremely high powered round as do some larger pistols. Remember that while you want enough power to stop an intruder, you don't want a high-powered round tearing through walls and endangering other family members.

High power is even a bigger problem with a rifle. Extremely powerful rifles can pierce walls easily and would be a particular hazard in an apartment complex. A long gun is also unwieldy.

But if your tastes run to long guns, a shotgun would be a better home defense weapon; some experts claim it is the best home defense weapon. A shotgun loaded with shot (not slugs) is less likely to pierce walls, and shoots a wider pattern than a rifle (although this could conceivably be a disadvantage in a situation where you must aim precisely; this is not a likely situation for home defense.)

The single-barrel shotgun, the least expensive kind, can be an utterly devastating weapon. For use in the home #6 birdshot can provide adequate stopping power without too much chance of wall penetration. This type

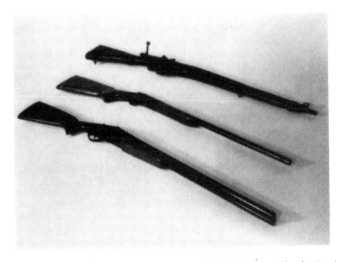

Rifles and shotguns. From top to bottom, an Enfield rifle, a Harrington/ Richardson single-barrel shotgun, and a Savage Springfield double-barrel shotgun.

of load will produce a 12-inch pattern at about 10 feet.

A double-barrel shotgun will provide two shots without the need to reload or recock. There are two triggers, each operating a barrel. Double barrel shotguns are expensive.

Automatic shotguns are also more expensive than the single-shot variety. They use the expanded gas to eject the spent shell and put another one in the firing position. This type of weapon can result in accidental firings in a stressful situation.

There's no question that preventing an intruder from entering your home is infinitely preferable to getting involved in a shootout. Arming yourself is not a cure-all for ending home breaks.

Chapter 14

An Ounce of Prevention

It seems as though we've been harping pretty heavily on prevention. After all, you don't find such a heavy dose of it in most self defense books. On the other hand, the glut of books on the market which stress prevention usually do so with nothing more than a brief mention of self defense.

The two concepts aren't mutually exclusive. Prevention is the first option in your self preservation arsenal; physical defense is the second.

Avoiding danger isn't a signal of cowardice—only of sound judgement. As a matter of fact, most people find that as their physical capabilities increase, they feel more comfortable about avoiding trouble, even to the point of walking away from a fight. The question of whether walking away is cowardly or simply good judgement will have to be answered in your own mind.

As you are well aware from reading the physical

defense chapters of this book, there are times when it's appropriate to walk away, times when it's reasonable to use gentle physical persuasion, and times when you should wade in and do as much damage as you can.

There are several methods of avoiding violence, but they all fall into two major categories: preventing trouble before it has a chance to start and cooling it off once it begins to brew. Prevention is the topic of this chapter; cooling things off will be examined in Chapter 15.

The beginning of this book gave a pretty comprehensive overview of prevention, but there are some areas which should be expanded. For one thing, we only briefly touched on the need to appear comfortable in your environment and not call attention to yourself in dangerous areas.

Now, let's do a personal inventory. It would be nice if someone could film you walking down the street, but barring that, have your spouse or someone else close to you give an *honest* appraisal. This may seem silly at first, but approach it with an open mind and you'll see why it's worthwhile.

Find answers to these questions:

☐ Do I have an unusual way of walking? Don't dismiss this lightly. A recent study found that a startling number of crime victims had an odd or stiff walk which apparently attracted attackers. It's not easy to change your gait, but it's not impossible, either. Actors and models often change their walking styles.

☐ Do I appear surly? Establishing eye contact with every passerby and cultivating a tough-guy image won't fool everybody, and will attract exactly the kind of attention you don't want.

☐ Do I appear alert? Someone staring blankly ahead is an attractive target.

☐ Does my body language give the impression that I am in control of myself and of my surroundings?

Think of the other aspects of your appearance and personality which might affect your susceptibility to crime. Try to change them if you can; if not, at least be aware of them.

Another point to consider is the fact that the tried-and-true crime prevention tips from law enforcement officials really do make sense. They won't make you invulnerable, but if you take these suggestions seriously you can improve your chances. Unfortunately, many people today are looking for easy answers and tend to ignore such maxims as traveling in groups rather than walking alone. They might not have this attitude, however, if they had read a piece of recent research which showed that criminals were more likely to go after a young, healthy man who was walking alone than for two older women. So the next time you're tempted to tune out the suggestions that have been offered for keeping yourself out of trouble, remember that you just might be stacking the deck against yourself.

There's a third aspect to preventing crime against you and your family, and it was briefly discussed in the home security chapter. When a neighborhood begins to go bad and crime rates rise, it begets more crime. If your neighbors are victimized, you stand a greater chance of being next.

Reporting suspects and suspicious activity—and, of course, crimes in progress—is critical to keeping a lid on crime. The effectiveness of this tactic depends on your local police department. Some departments are so severely understaffed that they may be lukewarm toward checking out someone who, for instance, is walking down the street with a TV set. (Yes, perhaps he is taking it to be repaired, or lending it to a neighbor, but he could be stealing it.)

Our basic impression, though, is that most police departments welcome such information from citizens, and in fact actually seek it. Leaders of crime prevention programs are well aware that only five to six percent of crimes that are discovered are actually discovered by police. The rest are discovered by citizens. To quote one crime prevention officer, "The eyes and ears of a concerned public are the most effective crime-fighting tool around."

One way citizens can use their eyes and ears to keep their neighborhood safe is by forming a crime watch program. These programs have, in some locations, proven very successful. Check with your local police department to find out more.

Chapter 15

Psychological Warfare

There's a fine line between a situation which can be handled with words and one which must be met with physical force. Generally speaking, as soon as an assailant lays a hand on you, you should respond physically, even if your response is something as simple as breaking the grip or otherwise removing his hand from your body.

But often there is a preliminary stage to a confrontation, a stage where hostilities are building and the situation is about to erupt.

In order to head off trouble, you will have to look for the warning signs of aggressive behavior in order to know exactly where you stand. If someone is shouting at you, pointing and gesturing, the situation may soon become violent, but the pointing and gesturing antagonist is not showing signs of immediate attack.

But when your antagonist begins to lean forward or

This posture indicates that he might be getting ready to unload on you. Be ready to throw a block and follow with a counterattack.

This man may be angry, but he's not in the process of getting ready to throw a punch.

draws one side of his body back, look out for a punch or other physical attack.

Other signs of imminent attack include the way your antagonist holds his hands. A balled fist is a sure sign of danger.

Knowing the state of mind of someone who is acting in an aggressive manner is a key to defusing a dangerous situation. If the situation is not too far advanced—if the person is not ready to strike you—psychological warfare can be your best weapon.

Your calm appearance is the biggest factor in cooling off an attacker. Fear is undoubtedly a factor for your attacker, too, regardless of his physical capabilities. Even the best fighters have butterflies before the first punch is thrown. It stands to reason that if the attacker feels a fear of you, he is less likely to follow through. The more you worry him, the less likely he is to start something.

What would make an attacker be afraid of you?

The fact that you're not afraid.

Put yourself in your attacker's shoes. If you were goading someone, trying to get a kick out of another person's fear, wouldn't you be worried if that person seemed totally unafraid, completely able to handle the situation?

Granted, you may be quaking on the inside, but following this strategy—giving the appearance of being unafraid—can work wonders.

It won't be easy, but consider the fact that if the attacker is intent on beating the daylights out of you and has the physical capability of doing it, he's going to beat you just as badly if you appear confident or if you appear terrified. He's not going to take pity on you because you're afraid! If he were the sensitive type, he wouldn't be beating people up in the first place. You have nothing to lose by maintaining a calm manner.

In a robbery situation, a calm appearance can be life-saving. A gun-toting robber might be a nervous wreck already, and any hysterical action on your part is going to make matters worse. Clamly hand over your money and don't panic. As stated earlier, never try to defend yourself against a gunman unless you have reason to believe he is about to shoot. (If, for instance, he has just cold-bloodedly gunned down your companion and is turning the gun on you.) When handling over your money, keep conversation to an absolute minimum, **because you will never know what will set your assailant off.**

Conversation—properly used—does have a place in self defense. The familiar situation of a fellow who is being aggressive for no apparent reason can sometimes be defused by asking, in a non-combative way, "Is there a problem? Is something bothering you?"

That question just might bring him to his senses. If it does, be prepared to drop the whole matter immediately. If it doesn't the situation is probably no worse than before.

Finally, consider bluffing. Theoretically, everything you do in a stressful situation is bluffing to some extent. Even the most cocky street slugger is bluffing, as is the swaggering cop and the hard-driving business-man.

Aside from the obvious bluffing technique of maintaining your calm appearance, a well-chosen statement might work, too. The key is to keep it short and believable. You might try something such as: "I won't tolerate being shoved and I'm perfectly able to make you stop." Don't go into a long history of the guys you've put in the hospital or your war exploits. Bragging loudly about your abilities in the martial arts could worsen the situation, but there's no reason why you couldn't give a simple statement about your knowledge of karate if you feel comfortable doing it.

Think about what you might say, how you would handle various situations, and plan in advance. Next to your attacker, panic will be your worst enemy.

Chapter 16

Conclusion

A wise man once noted that the function of fear is to warn us of danger, not to make us afraid to face it.

There may come a time when you must face a dangerous situation. If you can't control the fear that you feel, you will be conquered by panic, not by your attacker.

We hope that *Common Sense Self Defense* will help you develop the confidence you need to aproach danger wisely. You must not court danger, but you can't allow your life to be run by fear, either.

Use your fears to warn you of danger, and avoid trouble wherever you can. Learn to trust your instincts and good judgement because they are your best allies. When you can't avoid trouble, act decisively.

Perhaps this book has kindled a latent interest in physical development and the martial arts. Advanced training from a qualified instructor will help you work out some of the movements which you may have had difficulty grasping from the printed page.

In any event, we hope that you have benefitted from *Common Sense Self Defense*. We also hope that you never are confronted with the need to use the self defense techniques described.

Our foremost hope, however, is for Americans to be able to stop living in fear and simply get on with the business of living.